# The Adventure of Death

THE ADVENTURE OF DEATH

BY

ROBERT W. MACKENNA

M.A., M.D.

"To die will be an awfully big adventure"
JAMES M. BARRIE (*Peter and Wendy*)

G. P. PUTNAM'S SONS
NEW YORK AND LONDON
The Knickerbocker Press
1917

To
MY
FATHER AND MOTHER

FOREWORD

THE kindness and modesty of the author of this little volume have led him to ask me to write a preface for it, and I assent with much hesitation and diffidence.

There is probably no sensation which makes such universal and insistent appeal to intelligent beings as the anticipation of death. This anticipation manifests itself in a thousand different ways: between the ever-present and solemn dread of Dr. Johnson or Charles Wesley, or the calm and undaunted courage of James Wolfe or Captain Oates and the flippant cynicism of Vespasian or of Charles II, there are innumerable gradations of sensibility, but no one can altogether dismiss the idea.

The appeal then is universal, but perhaps at no time has it been more insistent than now, when millions of men and women of all nationalities are called upon to face death daily, and when not only they but all their kith and kin are sharing this anticipation on their behalf.

Few things can give us a more clear sense of the narrow limitations of our own powers than the consciousness of our inability to obtain even a glimpse of what lies immediately behind the veil, but it behoves everyone to form some clear conception of what lies on this side of it.

In this endeavour Dr. MacKenna's book will be found to render invaluable assistance. He has enjoyed exceptional opportunities, as a physician, of studying the state of mind and demeanour of those who are at the point of death, and of gathering and collating the experiences of soldiers who have faced the perils of war.

Those who are inclined to shun the contemplation of death from a vague sense of terror, may take heart from these pages, which certainly go far to proving that death itself is rarely a painful thing, although pain from other causes may attend it.

Foreword

"The fear of death," says Bacon, "as a tribute due to nature, is weak."

It is to be hoped that this little volume may, at the present time, give rise to discussion and to the collection of fresh evidence as to the sensations and experiences caused by the imminence of danger.

Dr. MacKenna's illustration of a large railway system (p. 44) is a most illuminating one, but there are other aspects of the subject which deserve investigation; for example, Does fear lie chiefly in the anticipation of pain rather than in facing an actually present peril? In the case of a soldier in battle, is not the fear of pain and death in some cases overmastered by the greater fear of disgrace or dereliction of duty?

Few men can have reached middle age without having had to face the prospect of death, either from some great and sudden peril or through the more deliberate process of, *e. g.*, a serious surgical operation.

If I may presume to draw upon my own

experience I would say that in face of sudden peril I have had no consciousness of fear, but for some time after it had passed, I was subject to a recurrent sense of shuddering at the narrowness of the escape, and what might have been the consequence. Is this a form of retrospective fear? In the case of an operation of which no one could foretell the result fear is undoubtedly present during the days of preparation, but when the patient is actually on the operating table this seems to pass away and to give place to a sensation of the inevitable, not unmixed with curiosity.

Be this as it may, I venture to hope that this volume will do much to clear up prevalent beliefs as to the Adventure of Death, and the reverent and confident spirit in which Dr. MacKenna treats the subject can hardly fail to bring comfort and reassurance to the faint-hearted.

JOHN MURRAY.

April, 1916.

PREFACE

THE subject dealt with in the following pages is one of interest to the whole human race, for some day each one of us must lay aside the avocations, big or little, that have occupied us, and pass through the portal that separates this life from the Unknown. It is part of the purpose of this book to show that the passage is not a painful experience, and that, as a rule, the most timid traveller divests himself of all fear when the shadow of the gateway looms over him.

These conclusions I have come to in the course of my work as a physician, and they are supported by almost all the members of my profession with whom I have discussed them, as well as by the large body of evidence available in literature and history. Your own great-hearted poet, Walt Whitman, who learned many lessons in his hospital work during the Civil War, has put this on record:—

"As to Death, it is in reality a very different affair from the romantic stage view of it. Death-bed speeches and scenes are of the rarest occurrence. I have witnessed hundreds of deaths, and, as a rule, it seems just a matter of course,—like having your breakfast, or any other event of the day, and met with indifference at the last, and with apathy or unconsciousness."

At the present time we in Europe are living in a welter of blood, and the Angel of Death is hovering over almost every household. Our young men go forth gladly, with a smile on their lips and high courage in their hearts, and very few have shunned the path of duty through any craven dread. They have discovered that to face Death is to learn to cease to fear him, and on the shell-torn battlefield many of them have readjusted their views of Life, of Death, and of the Beyond.

In the far-off days that preceded the war

few of us gave much thought to the ultimate ending of our lives, for, to every healthy man his own Death seems a remote contingency. But now our young men keep daily company with Death; he is always at their elbow, and they have found that his presence does not appal them. If we look at life aright we should recognize that their experience is our own, for even in the peaceful pursuits of the most sheltered life Death is never far off, and may at any moment lay a kindly hand upon the shoulder. I have sought to dissipate those dark and erroneous views that have gathered, like some chilling miasma, round the subject, and I am hopeful that what I have written may afford consolation and encouragement to the faint-hearted.

In the concluding chapters of the book I try to prove in the light of modern scientific knowledge that Death does not extinguish the life of the individual, but that we go on. This is a fundamental tenet of most religious systems, but, without appeal to revealed religion, I consider that we have reasonable grounds for believing that Death does not annihilate us, but that beyond the confines of this life we enter upon new and loftier experiences.

ROBERT W. MACKENNA.

LIVERPOOL, ENGLAND,
November, 1916.

CONTENTS

CHAPTER I
PROEM 3

CHAPTER II
THE GREAT ADVENTURE . . . 9

CHAPTER III
THE FEAR OF DEATH 27

CHAPTER IV
THE FEAR OF DEATH (*Continued*) . . 65

CHAPTER V
THE PAINLESSNESS OF DEATH . . 97

CHAPTER VI
EUTHANASIA 117

CHAPTER VII
WHAT LIFE GAINS FROM DEATH . . 129

CHAPTER VIII

DOES DEATH END ALL? (1) IS MAN MORE THAN MATTER? . . . 141

CHAPTER IX

DOES DEATH END ALL? (2) THE SURVIVAL OF PERSONALITY . . . 157

CHAPTER X

EPILOGUE 187

INDEX 191

CHAPTER I
PROEM

"Tota vita nihil aliud quam ad mortem iter est."
SENECA.

"Every day travels towards death, thy last only arrives at it."
MONTAIGNE.

"Life is but to do a day's work honestly, and death, to come home for a day's wages when the sun goes down."
WHYTE-MELVILLE.

CHAPTER I

PROEM

When, with his first cry, the new-born infant challenges the world, and sets out on his pilgrimage through life, he carries with him sealed orders. But whatever road he may have to travel, and be his journey long or short, there is one gate through which he must pass and one caravanserai in which, at last, he must take his rest:

"Nascentes morimur, finisque ab origine pendet."

No high-road to London is so thronged as that on which the new-born child sets his foot: for the whole human race is marching along it, and all the heroes of the romantic past, and the great men of ages yet unborn have travelled, or are still to travel, along that beaten highway. And there is no halting on the road. Day after day, night after night the crowd moves on. Men turn aside for a moment, for the business of life calls them, and there are treasures to be gathered by the way; or the shaded pleasaunces allure them for a little while; but ever the feet are turned to the same goal. The market-place, and the land of the lotos-eater are only roundabout paths through which the wayfarer may wander on his way to the inn at the journey's end. For we cannot build for ourselves any permanent abiding-place by the roadside.

Some of the travellers make better speed than others, and may reach the end of the journey within a moment or an hour of their setting out upon it. Others come to the end only when their hair is silvered and their eyes are dimmed; but for each the journey lasts a lifetime.

On, and on, and on, up the long, steep hill, and along the wearisome straight and down the slope into the valley, and onward and upward again go the myriad tramping feet—feet whose steps are as noiseless as those of ghosts, though they are the feet of living men. Thunder and rain, snow and the biting wind cannot hinder the progress of this great army, which moves relentless ever towards its goal; for the road of life is the road to death, and the caravanserai is the grave.

"Does the road wind uphill all the way?"
 "Yes, to the very end."
"Will the day's journey take the whole long day?"
 "From morn to night, my friend."

"But is there for the night a resting-place?"
 "A roof for when the slow dark hours begin."
"May not the darkness hide it from my face?"
 "You cannot miss that inn."

"Shall I meet other wayfarers at night?"
 "Those who have gone before."
"Then must I knock, or call when just in sight?"
 "They will not keep you standing at that door."

Proem

"Shall I find comfort, travel-sore and weak?"
"Of labour you shall find the sum."
"Will there be beds for me and all who seek?"
"Yea, beds for all who come."

CHAPTER II
THE GREAT ADVENTURE

"O eloquent, just and mighty Death! whom none could advise, thou hast persuaded; what none hath dared, thou hast done; and whom all the world hath flattered, thou only hast cast out of the world and despised; thou hast drawn together all the far-stretched greatness, all the pride, cruelty, and ambition of man, and covered it all over with these two narrow words,
Hic Jacet!"

SIR WALTER RALEIGH.

CHAPTER II

THE GREAT ADVENTURE

It is singular that though death has been a fact in human existence from the beginning of time, man's view of it has undergone very little change. That is because relatively little study or consideration has been devoted to it. The poets, the philosophers, and the great essayists like Montaigne and Bacon have toyed with the fringe of its garments, and have uttered high-sounding and imperishable words on the subtle mystery. But they are in a minority, and there are many men who do no more than fling an occasional thought to death with the same indifference as they would throw a bone to a dog. Very few, in any generation, have devoted to the fact of death the amount of reflection they dedicate to the every-day problems of life. For death is, they flatter themselves, a thing remote, while the present moment of life is urgent with duties. And in this age of motor-cars, and aviation, and quick transit by land and sea there is a danger of our losing, through lack of use, the faculty for reflection. We have no time to steal into some little nook of calm on the wayside of life for a quiet hour of thought. We are too busy throwing our moments away with prodigal hands to recognize that every one of them is a pearl of great price.

We have moved on since the days of our grandfathers, and on few topics to-day are our thoughts what theirs were.

Science has found the key to many mysteries; it has unlocked the secret of the colours of the rainbow; it has analysed the atmosphere of the sun, and weighed the world as in a balance; but it has not succeeded in putting death into its crucibles or test-tubes and explaining it; and to-day men stand as awe-stricken and puzzled in the presence of that great mystery as did our ancestors a thousand years ago.

To comprehend anything thoroughly we must be able to look at it from all sides. At present we can only regard death from the side, and in the light, of life.

Physical death is one of the penalties we pay for our individuality. When we pass low enough down in the scale of life we come upon a huge class of unicellular organisms, such as infusoria and many protozoa, which multiply by dividing into two, the parent organism being represented by two offspring, and so on through countless generations. The latest descendant has within its body some part of the original parent cell, and that fractional part is in some sense immortal. As Weismann says, "The individual life is short, but it ends not in death, but in transformation to two new individuals." But this is a poor starveling variety of immortality, and there are few men but would rather have their "crowded hour of glorious life" than enjoy the shadowy physical immortality of a protozoon.

Personally I should even prefer to have my allotted span of human life with all its capacities for joy and sorrow, and the caravanserai of the grave awaiting me at the end of the journey, than be called upon to endure the long-drawn-out vegetative existence of Adanson's Baobab tree at Cape Verde, which, he calculated, had braved the tempests of five thousand years.

None of us can escape death, for every avenue of life leads down to it, nor can we materially postpone the hour when we must arrive there. Applied sanitary science has done much in the last twenty years to lessen the death-rate throughout the country, and especially in our large cities. Fifty years ago the death-rate in London was twenty-four per thousand: to-day it has been reduced to fourteen; but all the prevention of preventible disease, the improvements in the water and milk supplies—which, if neglected, may become impetuous ministers of death—the better sanitation, and more modern methods of treating disease, have not succeeded in prolonging the average length of the individual life by more than two or three years. Civilization tends to take back with one hand what it gives with the other, and the high pressure at which life is lived to-day robs it of many of the advantages afforded by protection against the attack from without of the myrmidon germs of disease. And the small admitted gain in the length of human life is more apparent than real, for the average increase is, in large measure, made up from a diminution of infantile mortality in the first few years of life and by the prolongation of the lives of those who are born delicate.

In all ages there have been men who have lived far beyond the average duration of human life. St. Mungo, the patron saint of Glasgow, is reputed to have attained the ripe age of 185, and Thomas Parr was more than 150 years old when he died; and here and there one may meet or hear of a sporadic centenarian. But, in spite of exceptions, and in spite of all that science can do to ward off the advent of death, the words of Moses' sublime psalm still ring true: "The days of our years are three-score years and ten; and if by reason of strength they be fourscore years, yet is their strength labour and sorrow for it is soon cut off, and we fly away." The conclusion of the poet-prophet has been proved through all the intervening ages to be wonderfully true, despite the fact that it must have been formulated without reference to any carefully collated vital statistics.

In most cases a man's useful life ends with his seventieth year. After that he begins to view things in a wrong perspective. He has lost the zest of life; his enthusiasms have been whittled away by the edge of the years; he becomes a Jeremiah crying "Woe, woe," and prophesying strange dangers; or he drifts into senility and becomes an undiscerning *laudator temporis acti.* "And the strong men shall bow themselves . . . and they shall be afraid of that which is high, and fears shall be in the way . . . because man goeth to his long home."

From the beginning of time sorcerers and alchemists have sought to find an elixir of life which should keep man forever young, and be a prophylactic against death. The seekers are still with us, and are now represented by one of the foremost scientists of the day, Professor Élie Metchnikoff, of the Pasteur Institute, Paris. He has devoted much patient attention to the problem of the prolongation of life, and fancies that he has found a partial solution of it in the bacillus Bulgaricus—a potent strain of milk-souring bacillus—and the Glycobacter, from the intestine of the dog. But which of us, by drinking buttermilk, can add one span to the length of his days? and every year that passes sees a few more silver threads in the great scientist's hair, and he, too, like all things living, must some day pay the debt to Nature.[1]

"In the midst of life we are in death." It has been estimated that, in this world of ours, fifty-seven human beings die every minute of the day; and in addition there is an immense and incalculable mortality among all living creatures, insects, birds, and animals of every kind, besides plants and flowers. So that, though the fact rarely impinges upon our consciousness, we are every moment of our lives living in the valley of the shadow of death. And yet we find the world a very pleasant place to live in.

When Claude Bernard said *"La vie c'est la mort,"* he enunciated a great physiological truth, for every act of life is, in essence, an act of death. Every burning word that leaps from a poet's brain on to the virgin page, has come from some cell that in the throes of birth has given up some part of its vital force. Every gesture with which an

[1] Prof. Metchnikoff died on July 15, 1916, aged 71.

orator sways a multitude, is accompanied by the death of some cell or other in his body. Even the movement of my pen across the paper as I write means that cells are being broken down and destroyed in my hand and arm, and part of me is dying that, perchance, some other traveller on the road to death may find comfort on the way.

These processes of molecular death are taking place every moment in every one of us, and we are completely unconscious of them.

Each of us carries within him, from the moment of his birth, the subtle and malign mechanism that, if he escape disease or accident, will bring about his death. It is an elementary fact of bacteriology that many, if not all, micro-organisms produce as a by-product of their growth substances which are capable of destroying them. The classical example is the Saccharomyces or yeast-fungus, which, at a suitable temperature, grows luxuriantly in a solution of sugar.

But as it grows it converts the sugar into alcohol, and when the alcohol has reached a certain degree of concentration it kills the yeast-fungus. In no medium are the life and growth of the yeast-fungus more exuberant than in a solution of sugar: and in no other medium does it so rapidly compass its own death.

So it is with man. If he escape death from accident or from one of the diseases which all through life beset him like a pack of ravening wolves upon his flank, he dies ultimately of old age. And death from old age means, simply, the gradual poisoning of every cell in the body by long-continued exposure to the toxic substances that are produced within us by every act of life. In youth, and in the prime of manhood, these poisons are efficiently eliminated, and the body cells have a remarkable capacity for repair. But as the years pass on elimination becomes less and less effective, for the organs chiefly concerned with that function begin to succumb to the influence of the poisons they are called upon to discharge, and the retention of these toxic substances produces degenerative changes in every organ of the body, till the organs can no longer perform their functions properly, and the process culminates in death.

It is this poisoning of the system with the by-products of our physical life which causes fatigue after any great effort of mind or body. A sense of fatigue is nothing more than the subjective expression of auto-intoxication; and the disappearance of the sensation of fatigue after a Turkish bath, or a good sleep, indicates that satisfactory elimination of the poisonous by-products has been accomplished, and sleep has afforded the silent body-builders an opportunity to execute repairs.

Sleep itself is held by some physiologists to be the outcome of a toxæmia or poisoning, and the interesting fact that so many very old people sleep away the last few days of their lives indicates that in the manner of their death they are not far removed from the unicellular yeast-fungus.

Science has not yet succeeded in formulating an adequate definition of death. To define death simply as the cessation of vitality, is to define by negation, which is the refuge of the intellectually destitute. It has been defined as the loss of the capacity to respond to stimulation, but a curarized motor nerve or a sensory nerve "blocked" by cocaine is not dead, though its response to stimulation is temporarily in abeyance. When the influence of these drugs is removed the power of response is recovered. Still, as a working hypothesis, we may accept the definition, if we make the loss of capacity to respond permanent, though this definition will not satisfy those, who, like myself, believe that man is something more than matter. But, after all, the definition of death is of little account. The chief thing is that it is inevitable—part of that human destiny which we share with all our fellow-creatures.

"Licet quot vis vivendo vincere secla,
  Mors æterna tamen, nihilominus illa manebit."

We live our life among others. Indeed, our life consists of a series of events and circumstances in which others play a part. It is the merging into the lives of others, and the points of contact we make with them, that fashion or destroy much of our happiness here. We are gregarious: we live in a crowd, but we die alone. And out of this seeming loneliness of death man has evolved one of his objections to dying. It is here that the consolations of a robust religious faith nerve a man for the hazard.

Robertson of Brighton once said, "No man ever lived whose acts were not smaller than himself," and I have sometimes thought of these words when I have looked upon the face of the dead. There is a sublime dignity about death, and there are few faces that are not ennobled by its touch. For its marble hand smooths out the lineaments, and shows us the man as he really was. The furrows cut by the graving tool of care, the lines etched on the face by the acid of selfishness, and the wrinkles ploughed by the share of Time, are all obliterated or softened, and a quiet, impressive dignity settles on the face of the dead.

When Alexander Smith, the author of *City Poems*, said, "If you wish to make a man look noble, your best course is to kill him," he was guilty of a crude hyperbole; but, obviously, he had looked upon a dead face and seen, as others too have seen, the majesty and benignity of death. Max Müller had seen it when he wrote, "Never shall I forget the moment when for the last time I gazed upon the manly features of Charles Kingsley, features which death had rendered calm, grand, sublime. . . . There remained only the satisfied expression of triumph and peace, as of a soldier who had fought a good fight and who, while sinking into the stillness of the slumber of death, listens to the distant sounds of music and to the shouts of victory. One saw the ideal man, as Nature had meant him to be, and one felt that there is no greater sculptor than Death."

CHAPTER III
THE FEAR OF DEATH

"Optanda mors est, sine metu mortis mori."

SENECA.

"Cowards die many times before their death,
 The valiant never taste of death but once."

SHAKESPEARE.

"He who has learned to die, has forgot what it is to be a slave."

MONTAIGNE.

"The most rational cure, after all, for the inordinate fear of death is to set a just value on life."

WILLIAM HAZLITT.

CHÁPTER III

THE FEAR OF DEATH

It is a remarkable fact, which Metchnikoff describes as one of the disharmonies of life, that, as we rise in the animal world, the aversion to and fear of death increases. Low down in the scale there are animals which can witness the death of their fellows without the slightest evidence of comprehending that a like fate awaits them some day. But, higher up, among the mammals there are others which manifest acute fear when confronted with the dead bodies of their own kind. Most horses, for example, are obviously distressed and frightened when brought face to face with a dead member of their own species. But we may well doubt whether any animal, however highly developed, is possessed of the knowledge that death is inevitable. That knowledge is one of the penalties which man must pay for his higher development.

Rousseau, with brutal frankness, said, "He who pretends to face death without fear is a liar." But he was a philosopher of unhealthy mind and morbid habits, and should not be accepted as an infallible authority upon the matter. Tolstoy, in his later years, came nearer to the truth when he said, "No one is afraid of falling asleep, and yet the phenomena of sleep are like those of death—there is the same loss of consciousness. Man does not fear sleep, although the arrest of consciousness is as complete as in death." The comparison is a fair one, but there is a tiny flaw running through it, for we know from the experience of ourselves and others that sleep is but a temporary condition, and that when it is over we return again to the full consciousness of life. Still, as Donne wrote, we

"Practise dying by a little sleep,"

and every time we fall asleep we perform a sublime experiment of faith. Sleep is, in the quaint words of Sir Thomas Browne: "In fine, so like death, I dare not trust it without my prayers, and an half adieu unto the World, and take my farewell in a colloquy with God."

I do not believe that the fear of death is a natural instinct. It is not something inborn in us like hunger or thirst, else all little children would possess it. I believe, rather, that it is a mental attribute which has been developed, in process of evolution, for the protection of the species. It is one of those acquisitions that have promoted the survival of the fittest, and it is a factor of incalculable value in the whole order of things. Without the fear of death the gateway to suicide would be thrown open, and the coward heart would seek escape from every difficulty of life by destroying it. It is said that Hegesias painted the miseries of life in such dark colours that many of his pupils chose death as the less sombre alternative. But, for most of us, life has so much to offer that we are never tempted to throw it away, and the salutary fear of the Unknown which lies beyond the gate of death makes us wonderfully tolerant of "the slings and arrows of outrageous fortune."

Shakespeare, with his splendid sanity, has stated the problem for all time:

"For who would bear the whips and scorns of time,
  The oppressor's wrong, the proud man's contumely,
  The pangs of despised love, the law's delay,
  The insolence of office, and the spurns
  That patient merit of the unworthy takes,
  When he himself might his quietus make
  With a bare bodkin? Who would fardels bear,
  To grunt and sweat under a weary life,
  But that the dread of something after death

.   .   .   .   . puzzles the will,
And makes us rather bear those ills we have,
Than fly to others that we know not of?"

Finot has said that "man himself created the fear of death," but whether or not this be true we cannot escape from the conclusion that man has heightened and increased the fear by the pageantry of funereal gloom with which he has surrounded death. There comes back to me the memory of an incident in my childhood which, analysed in the light of later experience, indicates from what sources we derive our gloomy, fearful views of death. In an old white house, separated by a field from the home of my childhood, lived a venerable old gentleman. I remember him well, after the long lapse of years. He was, I think, fond of children, and whenever he met me on the road he had a cheery greeting and, on occasion, would conjure up a sweet from some mysterious recess of his coat-pocket. He died suddenly. I do not think his death caused me the least sorrow.

I had a childish faith that all good people go to heaven, and a kind old gentleman who carried sweets in his pocket would certainly not be denied entrance to that happy land. I imagined him, as I had last seen him, with his large white hat, walking about the streets in heaven giving sweets to small angels. He was dead; but he had gone to heaven, so what was the need of tears.

Four days after his death I was playing in the field which separated his house from ours, on a slope beside a hawthorn tree which still stands, when the sound of the muffled padding of lightly shod hoofs drew my attention from my play. Up the long avenue to the house there was coming a terrible apparition—a long, black coach, the top of which was surmounted by great black nodding plumes, drawn by two black horses with sweeping tails, and driven by a solemn-faced man from whose black hat a long streamer of crêpe fluttered in the wind. It was an old-fashioned funeral hearse. I had never seen one before, but the sight of it in some inexplicable way froze my heart, and it was as though a black cloud had passed across the face of the sun. It was my first vision of the gloom of death, and I felt a strange desire to cry. I could no longer think of my old friend as happy in heaven. In some way this dreadful thing I had seen was associated with him, and death had ceased to be a safe transition from earth to heaven and had become a thing black, mysterious, and awesome.

And so deeply do some of the memories of pain cut their impress upon the plastic heart of a child, that I never revisit that field and pass beneath the branches of the hawthorn tree without recalling and revisualizing the whole scene. I can still hear the muffled beating of hoofs, and see the black and nodding plumes.

We have abolished some of the funereal gloom from the chamber of death since the days of Bacon. We no longer hang the walls and drape the death-bed with black, and we make a larger use of the gentle ministry of flowers, but we may still say with him:

" Pompa mortis magis terret quam mors ipsa."

It must be admitted that the fear of death is very widely disseminated among men; but it is not a deep-rooted instinct, or it would not be so readily overcome. It is the least of fears. It gives way before many sudden emotions or impulses such as love, the excitement of battle, the call of duty, religious devotion, and the maternal instinct. When a sudden and imperious call comes to men or women to risk their lives for some tender object of their affection, the fear of death is thrown roughly to the wall.

After the South African War I had many opportunities of talking the matter over with some of the men who fought through it, and I obtained ample confirmation of the opinion which I had already formed from my reading, that, in the heat of battle, the fear of death is absolutely obliterated. These men told me that the most testing time was the five minutes before the action began. Then there was tense anxiety, and a curious sense of uncertainty, sometimes accompanied by a feeling of thirst; but once the heavy guns had commenced to roar their challenge, and hurl their death-pealing shells, all fear of death was forgotten, swallowed up in the excitement of battle. Even the wounding or death of a comrade close by, did not suffice to reawaken the dread of death, and some who were wounded have told me that at the moment of their injury they were unaware that they had been hurt, and did not realize that they were stricken men till they were overcome by weakness. But after the fight was over, and the din of battle had ebbed into a great and vague silence, as they lay on the veldt and longed for the arrival of the ambulance-men, worn out by loss of blood and tortured by thirst, they tasted in apprehension the bitterness of death.

The conditions of warfare on the Continent

at the present moment differ considerably from those which have prevailed in any preceding war. The fighting is more continuous, and the shell-fire more deadly and attended by more terror-provoking accompaniments than any to which our soldiers have hitherto been exposed. But these circumstances have failed to blast the courage of our men with the fear of death. I have questioned many of them closely, immediately after their return from the front, while the impressions of battle were still lurid in their memory, and in no case have I discovered that the fear of death ever crossed their mind once they were in the thick of the fight. Most of those with whom I have talked admitted that just before they went into the fighting-line they felt a little nervous, but not more nervous than they had felt on many a less serious occasion.

The average Briton is not given to introspection. His capacity for analyzing his emotions varies with the quantity of Celtic blood in his veins. A Lowland Scot or a soldier from the midlands of England will give a much more reticent and superficial account of his feelings when in battle, than will a Scottish Highlander, a Welshman, or an Irishman. But yet, in the main, there is a singular unanimity about their conclusions. Practically all admit that they felt some apprehension for their personal safety on their way to the firing line for the first time. A young Welsh officer told me quite frankly that when he first came under shell-fire he felt tempted to turn and run; but he was arrested by the thought that he must set his men a good example, and this spirit of *noblesse oblige* which has saved the honour of our Empire upon many a stricken field enabled him to steady himself and stick to his post. How this traditional spirit of the British officer reacts upon his men was made clear to me by a Gordon Highlander who was inured to battle on the retreat from Mons. He confessed to a feeling of extreme uneasiness until he noticed how calmly and collectedly the officers were going about their duties. He drew immediate encouragement from this observation, and made up his mind that, come what might, no action of his should tarnish the honour of his regiment. At a later date he received promotion for consistently brave conduct in the field, and, though many times in very dangerous situations, he assured me that no fear of death or anxiety for his personal safety ever worried him after his first baptism of fire. He was severely wounded by machine-gun fire at Neuve Chapelle, and as he lay in the "no-man's-land" between the opposing trenches he had so little thought of danger that he raised himself on his elbow to admire and applaud the magnificent charge of a territorial battalion of his regiment. His movements apparently attracted the attention of an enemy sniper, and the arm on which he had raised himself was shattered, but even then he felt no fear of death.

An artillery officer, whose battery was hopelessly outranged, told me that his feelings, when he saw his friends and gunners being blown to pieces by the high-explosive shells that were raining upon them, were not those of anxiety for himself or regret at the fate of his friends. That came later, when he missed them at the mess-table. So far as he could analyse his emotions he believed that his one feeling was that of furious anger at being unable to retaliate.

One soldier, a dark-haired Celt, had a very lively recollection of all the events which immediately preceded his first entry into the fire-trench. The prospect of facing danger had the effect of quickening all his faculties of perception, and he told me that, as he marched to the trenches, every blade of grass seemed to have become a more vivid green; every wayside flower was clothed with a fresh beauty; the warbling of the birds was sweeter than he had ever heard it before, and the little fleecy clouds in the sky were as white as driven snow. He wondered, as he went, if he should live to see and hear these things on the morrow. He wondered whether he would be killed; and what it would be like to die. He hoped that if he were to be killed his death would be instantaneous. He visualized himself dead. He thought of his friends at home, of incidents of his boyhood and his early manhood. Then, as he walked, he prayed; and he found that the prayer he was repeating in a whisper was not a prayer specially formulated for the occasion, but was a simple string of petitions which he had learned as a little child.

We can well imagine that, to a man with such an introspective and sensitive mind, the actual experience of being under fire would be trying in the extreme; but, as a matter of fact, he found it less formidable than he expected; and, in analysing his feelings after his first spell of duty in the trenches, he could not recall any memory of fear. His chief feeling seems to have been one of acute irritation at the nerve-racking noise of shell-fire. Not a few soldiers have assured me that the noise of an artillery bombardment has caused them more distress than any other experience they have gone through, and one hardy Tyneside collier, who had been through much of the severe fighting on the peninsula of Gallipoli, told me that he had never had the least fear of death, but he always dreaded and shuddered at the noise of the big naval guns, and the reverberating concussion of exploding shells. On thinking his statement over, I came to the conclusion that, in all probability, his distress of mind on hearing a shell burst was due to the fact that in the life of a collier an explosion all too often means the entombment and death, by fire or asphyxiation, of many brave men. An explosion in a coal-pit is a danger which a collier faces daily. Though, probably, the fear of such explosions is not perpetually before him, the possibility of such an occurrence, with its hideous train of casualties, is always lurking in his subconscious mind. We are all prone to measure new experiences by old standards. From his boyhood this man had been accustomed to regard an explosion as a frightful calamity, and explosions on the field of battle awakened in his mind precisely the same feelings as would the thought of such a catastrophe in his coal-pit.

An officer who had seen much heavy fighting told me, without the slightest suggestion of boasting, that he had thoroughly enjoyed every day at the front, and was anxious to get back to the thick of the fighting again. Before the war he had been for several months on a big-game shooting expedition. Much of his life had been occupied with adventure, and he regarded the war as a superior kind of sport. He had never felt the slightest fear either of wounds or death; and he was of opinion that in the hurricane of battle even a craven becomes a brave man.

The truth seems to be that as the danger of death increases, the fear of it recedes. As in other paths of life, familiarity breeds contempt, and the anxiety which a young soldier feels on his first visit to the trenches rapidly gives way to a stolid indifference. Men become so inured to the hazards of war that they can actually play practical jokes on each other and on their enemies in the shell-torn, bullet-swept trenches.

Whatever apprehensions a soldier may confess to having experienced on the way to battle, there is but one verdict as to the effect of the ordeal, and that is that every element of fear for one's personal safety is completely obliterated. To wait in the reserve trenches would seem to be much more nerve-racking than to be in the forefront of the fight. The fact seems to be that the mind is so occupied with the business in hand that there is no room for any thought of fear to obtrude itself.

How this comes about may best be shown

by an illustration. Let us imagine that the brain—the organ which links up the body with the sources of thought and action—is a railway terminus, into which run lines from all parts of the country. There are lines to and from the eyes, the ears, the feet, the hands, and every muscle in the body. In the heat of battle, trains loaded with messages are running from every outlying station in the body to the terminus, while other trains laden with messages are racing on the down line to every muscle. On a well-ordered railway system certain trains have priority; while others are held back till the congestion of traffic is relieved and some of the metals are cleared. A wise station-master will see that a slow goods train does not get in the way and block the progress of a passenger express; and the mind, acting in this rôle, takes care that no train laden with fear finds its way out of the terminus to throw the other traffic into confusion. There are no metals to spare for such a cargo; the whole railway system is occupied with the supply of more urgent necessities.

By a similar illustration one can explain the frequently repeated observation that in the heat of battle a soldier may sustain a formidable wound, and feel no pain whatever, and even be unaware that he has been hit. The injured limb or organ despatches an express train along the line of some sensory nerve to the railway terminus in the brain; but on drawing near the terminus the signals are found to be against it, and it cannot force its way through the press of traffic into the station. It is therefore sidetracked. But just as an ordinary train will try to call the attention of the signalman by blowing its whistle when the signal is against it, so a sensation of pain may succeed in calling the attention of the brain to its existence by sending on a message not of pain, but of heaviness or pressure. This may have the effect of opening a path for the whole train to run through, and the wounded man begins to discover he has been hit and hurt. But in many cases a long interval elapses between the infliction of a wound and the realization by the sufferer that he has been wounded.

I have been informed by a soldier who had a large piece blown out of the side of his thigh, that he was quite unaware of his injury for several minutes. His attention was attracted by hearing his foot "squelch" every time he moved it. On looking down he saw that his boot was full of blood; then, almost immediately, he felt a dull ache in his thigh, followed very shortly by a sensation of acute pain. In his case, to return to our illustration, the messages of pain from his wounded thigh had been held up by the congestion of traffic near the terminus. We may imagine that the impeded train endeavoured to call the attention of the signalman, but failed to do so until a message, sent from the suburban station of Sight, not far from the terminus, got through, and informed the station-master that a very important train from a remote part of the country was being held up. The levers were then at once drawn, and the sensation of pain passed on to the sensorium.

The illustration is a somewhat mechanical one, and may not satisfy either the physiologist or the psychologist, but it will help to explain certain curious phenomena that have frequently provoked surprise.

It is impossible to imagine a more trying experience than participation in a bayonet charge; but yet over and over again I have been assured that no fear enters a soldier's mind when he is taking part in one. A soft-voiced, quiet-looking soldier, who had returned home wounded, after taking part in no less than seven bayonet charges, informed me that he had never felt the slightest fear when engaged in this deadly work. He had no time to think of self. His orders were to storm a certain position, and he had done so. Other men have told me that they "saw red," as they leaped over the trench parapet with bayonets fixed. This "seeing red" is probably more than a mere phrase, and may be due to a tremendous engorgement of the vessels of the retina or the visual centre with blood in consequence of the great emotional strain of the moment; but in no case has any soldier admitted to me that he felt the least fear of death, when, bayonet on rifle, he raced over the bullet-swept zone towards the opposing trench.

The truth seems to be that in the frenzy of battle the soldier is affected by a kind of mental exaltation, a detachment from self, which renders him impervious to any thought of personal danger.

". . . . . . Corpora bello
Objectant, pulchramque petunt per vulnera
    mortem."

But even at a distance from the din of battle, and without the excitement which it begets, the call of duty can overcome the fear of death.

We have a daily illustration of this afforded by the conduct of the firemen in our great cities, or the resolute lifeboat men round our inhospitable coasts who are always ready, without flinching, to put their lives to the hazard in the performance of their tasks. And that higher sense of duty which blossoms into loyalty to a cause, or to one's friends, has enabled many a man to sacrifice his life without fear. Somewhere near the Franco-Belgian frontier is the grave of a nameless hero whose devotion to his comrades enabled him to overcome the fear of death. The story is best told in the simple narrative of one of his fellow-soldiers:

"He was one of our men, a private in the Royal Irish Regiment. We learned that he had been captured the previous day by a party of German cavalry, and had been held a prisoner at the farm where the Germans were in ambush for us. He tumbled to their game, and though he knew that if he made the slightest sound they would kill him, he decided to make a dash to warn us of what was in store. He had more than a dozen bullets in him, and there was not the slightest hope for him. We carried him into a house until the fight was over, and then we buried him next day with military honours. His identification disc and everything else was missing, so that we could only put over his grave the tribute to a Greater:

'He saved others: himself he could not save.'

There wasn't a dry eye among us when we laid him to rest in that little village."

When the world was thrilled by the news of the appalling disaster to the *Titanic*, horror gave way to pride as we heard how many a man and woman on that doomed ship, touched by the finger of catastrophe, was transmuted from common clay into pure and heroic gold. But few stories in that record of noble deeds caught the popular imagination as did the plain tale of the Marconi operator, who, though one of the first on the stricken liner to know what her fate must be, stuck at his post and sent message after message through the midnight air to summon help that came only too late. He kept on performing his duty calmly, until his cabin was flooded and his instruments could send messages no longer, holding his life a very little thing, and the fear of death of none account while his duty had to be done.

But probably it is in the nursing and medical professions that one will find the most plentiful illustrations of the fact that the call of duty can overcome the fear of death. In their daily work nurses and doctors are continually exposed to personal danger, yet such is the strength of their sense of duty that no consideration of risk enters into their calculations when plague or pestilence has to be faced. They will be careful, as far as possible, to protect themselves from infection, but they will not be held back from their duty, trembling and afraid, by any craven fear of death.

Thanks to the epoch-making discovery of diphtheritic antitoxin by Behring and Roux we do not now see so many of those appalling cases of laryngeal diphtheria which used to asphyxiate little children as with the ruthless fingers of some strangling Thug, or if we do meet with them we are not so powerless to combat them. But before the days of antitoxin, and even since then, many a nurse or doctor, at grave personal risk, has sucked the diphtheritic membrane from a child's throat, and made no boast of it. For before the face of duty the fear of death shrinks into a very little thing.

In November, 1898, at the Allgemeines Krankenhaus in Vienna—at that time the largest hospital in Europe—a tragedy occurred which deserves to be commemorated in letters of gold. Some time previously a Commission of Austrian doctors had been at work in India investigating bubonic plague. They brought home with them a quantity of plague bacilli, and a series of experiments upon animals was instituted to discover, if possible, the way in which the disease was propagated, and to seek for a remedy.

A laboratory attendant contracted plague in a very virulent form, and a young doctor, Hermann Müller, whom the man had been assisting, voluntarily undertook the duty of looking after him. He was assisted by two nurses who also volunteered. The man died, and Dr. Müller not only placed him in his coffin, but personally undertook the duty of disinfecting the room in which he had expired. In this, his ardour outran his discretion, for he scraped the plaster off the walls and ceiling of the room, a precaution which was quite unnecessary, as the same end could have been achieved by a powerful antiseptic spray, or by thorough fumigation. While doing this he must necessarily have inhaled much infected dust. When his task was completed he isolated himself for a period, and during this time he himself discovered with the microscope, in the matter which he coughed up from his lungs, a large number of plague bacilli. He had developed plague in its deadliest form. He knew that he was a doomed man. He locked the door of his room; wrote a letter to his "chief" announcing the fact that he had contracted plague in its pneumonic form, and saying that as he had only a few days to live he hoped no one would expose himself to danger by coming to his aid; wrote another pathetic little note of farewell to his parents, and, having pushed his missives under the door, where they were found next day, lay down on his bed to die. He had done his duty, and in doing it had overcome the terror of death. To the eternal credit of his profession let it be said that he was not left to die alone.

Another luminous example comes to mind. Dr. Arthur Frame Jackson, a young man of great promise, arrived in China, whither he had gone as a medical missionary, just at the time when a severe epidemic of bubonic plague was driving the panic-stricken peasants in a wild stampede before it. It was necessary, that the pestilence might be controlled, that this stampede should be arrested, and that only natives free from all signs of disease, and with no record of contact with plague-stricken persons, should be allowed to pass through the cordon. Jackson volunteered for the work of inspection, and, with no thought of self, but with that fine loyalty to duty which all who knew him expected from him, spent his days and nights in the arduous and dangerous work of examining suspects. He contracted plague and died, but his name will always live in the annals of medicine as one of that long line of brave men for whom death had no fears, because duty called.

A well-grounded, firmly established religious faith is the best possession for a man's last hours, and in the consuming flame of religious devotion which kindles so many illumined lives the fear of death is shrivelled up like a vagrant moth.

Father Damien dedicated his life to the service of the lepers on the island of Molokai, fought with death, faced death, and lived with death in that remote charnel-house every day for years, and died a leper. And in many of the darkest places of earth, far from home and kindred, and in daily peril of death there are men and women who dedicate their lives fearlessly to the service of God and humanity, because an altar fire of religious faith burns in their souls.

Out of the pages of martyrology we can gather many proofs that religious faith can overcome the fear of death. Take, for instance, the case of Archibald Campbell, first Marquis of Argyll. He was found guilty of "high treason"—a comprehensive term in those days—and sentenced to death by beheading at the Cross of Edinburgh on May 27th, 1661. All through life he had been a somewhat nervous and timid man, but after his condemnation he said, "I am as content to be here," among the prisoners in the Tolbooth, "as in the Castle, and I was as content in the Castle as in the Tower of London, and there I was as content as when at liberty; and I hope to be as content upon the scaffold as in any of them all."

Faith triumphed over fear, and to the very end of life he bore himself with a gallant equanimity. He slept with the utmost composure during the two nights that intervened between his sentence and its execution, as was proved by David Dickson, who shared his cell. On the scaffold, which he mounted without trepidation, he was perfectly unperturbed. His physician felt his pulse and found it beating at the usual rate, regularly and strongly. A preacher in the surrounding crowd, George Hutcheson by name, called to him, "My Lord, hold your grip siccar." "Mr. Hutcheson," Argyll replied, "You know what I said in the chamber, *I am not afraid to be surprised with fear.*"

And so he died, giving with his own hand the signal for the fall of the knife. He was boot." When lying under sentence he said, "I am not so cumbered about dying as I have often been about preaching a sermon," and his last words were, "Welcome Death."

The story of the burning of Ridley and Latimer is a *locus classicus* in martyrology. The evening before his death Ridley's brother offered to watch with him all night. "No, no," he replied, "I shall go to bed, and, God willing, shall sleep as quietly to-night as ever I did in my life." Next day, side by side with Latimer, chained to the same stake, over against the hoary pile of Balliol College, Ridley was burned to death; and his companion's words are still as redolent of the flower of bravery as the day they were spoken: "Be of good comfort, Master Ridley, and play the man; we shall this day light such a candle, by God's grace, in England, as I trust shall never be put out."

And there was no fear in the heroic heart of Archbishop Cranmer, when, girdled with

The Fear of Death

man who, on the admission of himself and
s contemporaries, was of a nervous disposi-
on, but his religious faith enabled him to
ercome the fear of death.

James Guthrie, another martyr of the
ood-red Scottish Covenanting times was
nged at the Cross of Edinburgh less than
week after the execution of Argyll. On
e morning of his execution, when asked
w he felt he said, "Very well, this is the
y which the Lord hath made; let us be
d and rejoice in it." When on the scaffold
said, "I take God to witness, I would not.
change this scaffold with the palace or the
tre of the greatest prelate in Britain."

In the pages of *Old Mortality* there is a
ricature, unworthy of the magic pen of
Walter, of a young Covenanting preacher
led the Rev. Ephraim Macbriar. The
ototype of this character has been identi-
d by authorities as Hugh Mackail, who
s martyred in his thirty-sixth year after
luring the unspeakable torture of "the

fire, he thrust his right hand into the flames crying, "That unworthy right hand."

Every country and every age has had its martyrs for their faith; and an impartial study of the records must persuade even the most incredulous that religious devotion is the strongest antidote to the fear of death.

When brought into conflict with a deep-rooted natural endowment such as the maternal instinct the acquired fear of death, however overpowering it may be in relation to the other facts of life, is utterly vanquished. The maternal instinct is latent in every woman, and, however well concealed it may be underneath the multifarious activities of the modern daughter of Eve, it is ready to spring into vitality at the call of love. For some women motherhood must always be a perilous experience, fraught with danger and attended by much suffering; but I have never known a woman, happily married, of her own free will permanently refuse to wear her crown, even though it should prove to be a crown of thorns worn on the way to the grave. When in general practice I was privileged to pilot many women through their hour of anguish into a haven of great joy; and sometimes it was necessary to warn them that a similar adventure could not be embarked upon without great danger to their life. They listened, and, apparently, took the warning to heart; but in some instances, after a few years, either the desire for another child to be a companion to the first, whose loneliness they grieved at, or the ache in the empty heart from which death had stolen the delight of their eyes, obliterated all memory of the warning, and their feet went down to death again that they might fulfil the noblest destiny of their sex. There is no halo on their brow, there is no Victoria Cross on their breast, and they pass unnoticed and unknown along our city streets; but no soldier-hero can teach them bravery, nor any martyred saint contempt of death.

CHAPTER IV
THE FEAR OF DEATH (*continued*)

"There is pain and sorrow enough in the world for us to spare investing death with grim terrors of our own. There is no terror to the dying about death at all."

A. C. BENSON.

"So live, that when the summons comes to join
  The innumerable caravan, that moves
To that mysterious realm where each shall take
His chamber in the silent halls of death,
Thou go not like the quarry slave at night
Scourged to his dungeon; but sustained and soothed
By an unfaltering trust, approach thy grave
Like one that wraps the drapery of his couch
About him, and lies down to pleasant dreams."

WILLIAM CULLEN BRYANT.

CHAPTER IV

THE FEAR OF DEATH (*continued*)

WHEN a normal man is in perfect health he has, undoubtedly, in some degree, a salutary fear of death. This fear is the protest of his vitality against its extinction. But, when his hour comes, I am firmly convinced that in almost every case the fear is lost.

We can adduce evidence in support of this opinion from three sources: (1) The witness of history; (2) the testimony of those who have been threatened by apparently inevitable death, and escaped; and (3) the evidence supplied by those who, in the course of their work, have seen many people die.

In great measure the intensity with which men fear death is a matter of temperament.

All through life Dr. Samuel Johnson was a meticulous valetudinarian obsessed by the fear of death. Once, when Boswell asked him, "Is not the fear of death natural to man?" Johnson replied, "So much so, sir, that the whole of life is but keeping away the thought of it." Over and over again in the immortal pages of his carefully chronicled small-talk we are reminded of his shrinking dread of death. He shrank from it partly through fear of the physical act of dissolution, and partly because he stood in awe of the fate that might await him after death. He once quarrelled violently with his biographer, who persisted in discussing the subject. Boswell ventured to ask him: "But may we not fortify our minds for the approach of death?" In a passion, Johnson thundered, "No, sir, let it alone! It matters not how a man dies, but how he lives. The act of dying is not of importance, it lasts so short a time." But when Boswell, with that pertinacity which is half his passport to immortality, returned to the theme, Johnson lost his temper and roared, "Give us no more of this! Don't let us meet to-morrow."

On Easter Monday, 1784, a few months before his end came, he wrote to his friend, the Reverend Dr. Taylor, "O! my friend, the approach of death is very dreadful. I am afraid to think on that which I know I cannot avoid."

And yet, in spite of this grisly horror of death that had haunted him all his days, he died bravely and unafraid. During his last illness he asked his physician, Dr. Brocklesby, to tell him whether he could recover, and insisted on an unequivocal answer. On learning that, so far as human knowledge could tell, there was no hope of recovery, he said, "Then I will take no more physic, not even my opiates; for I have prayed that I may render up my soul to God unclouded." He refused all alcoholic stimulants for the same reason. At the end he passed through the great portal without a trace of fear. Cawston, who sat with him the night before he died, bore witness that "no man could appear more collected, more devout, or less terrified at the thoughts of the approaching minute," and he breathed his last so peacefully "that his attendants hardly perceived when his dissolution took place."

There was no fear in Anne Boleyn's heart when she said, "The executioner is, I hear, very expert, and my neck is very slender," and she put her hands round her neck and laughed heartily; nor in the words with which Sir Thomas More addressed his friends as he ascended the scaffold: "See me safe up, for my coming down I can shift for myself." As Addison wrote, "He maintained the same cheerfulness of heart upon the scaffold which he used to show at his table; and upon laying his head on the block gave instances of that good humour with which he had always entertained his friends in the most ordinary occurrence. His death was of a piece with his life. There was nothing in it new, forced, or affected. He did not look upon the severing his head from his body as a circumstance that ought to produce any change in the disposition of his mind; and, as he died under a fixed and settled hope of immortality, he thought any unusual degree of sorrow and concern improper to such an occasion as had nothing in it which could deject or terrify him."

There were features of dramatic grandeur about the execution of Sir Walter Raleigh. He was a man of extraordinary diversity of character; a courtier, a brave adventurer accustomed to put his life to the hazard on sea and land, a historian in the leisure of his prison days, and something of a poet. In addition, his outlook on life was that of a philosopher, and he was deeply religious. That he loved life is proved by the strenuous way in which, shaking with ague but not fear, he pleaded his cause at his trial. He heard sentence of death pronounced on him without flinching, and when taken back to his cell remarked philosophically, "The world itself is but a larger prison out of which some are daily selected for execution." We catch an echo of the secret of his brave and undaunted spirit in his beautiful lines:

"Give me my scallop-shell of quiet,
　My staff of truth to walk upon,
My scrip of joy, immortal diet,
　My bottle of salvation:
My gown of glory, Hope's true gage,
And thus I'll take my pilgrimage."

In his "Narrative of the last hours of Sir Walter Raleigh," that industrious *chiffonnier*, that quaint collector of unconsidered but priceless trifles, Isaac Disraeli, says: "Rawleigh's cheerfulness was so remarkable and his fearlessness of death so marked, that the Dean of Westminster, who attended him, at first wondering at the hero, reprehended the lightness of his manner, but Rawleigh gave God thanks that he had never feared death, for it was but an opinion, and an imagination; and, as for the manner of death, he would rather die so than of a burning fever; and that some might have made shows outwardly, but he felt the joy within. The dean says that he made no more of his death than if he had been going to take a journey."

On the morning of his execution his spirits were at their highest, and he was brimful of a kindly humour. He died with a grand air; embracing his executioner, who knelt to ask his forgiveness; examining the axe with the scrutiny of a connoisseur, and, as he laid it down remarking, "This is a sharp medicine, but a sound cure for all diseases." Then he commended himself to God, desiring the crowd of spectators to pray for him, and laid his neck upon the block; and when the executioner, unnerved by the fine nobility and quiet courage of his victim, hesitated to perform his task, it was Raleigh's calm imperative "Strike, man!" that urged him to the deed. One of the contemporary letter-writers quoted by Disraeli says, "In all the time he was upon the scaffold, and before, there appeared not the least alteration in him, either in his voice or countenance, but he seemed as free from all manner of apprehension as if he had been come thither rather to be a spectator than a sufferer." He died in the grand manner of his time, a courtier, and a gallant Christian gentleman.

During the last uneasy years of his life Oliver Cromwell was obsessed by melancholy and strange anxieties; but his dying words show that whatever fear he had of man, he had none of death. "My desire," he said, "is to make what haste I may to be gone."

When Queen Mary II was dying she said to Archbishop Tillotson, who had paused in reading a prayer, "My Lord, why do you not go on? I am not afraid to die," words which found a singular echo in the last utterance of Charles Darwin, who, with his last breath, said, "I am not in the least afraid to die."

When John Sterling, at the close of a

short and somewhat sorrowful life, lay dying, he wrote a letter of farewell to his friend Carlyle, of which Mr. A. C. Benson, says, "In its dignity, its nobleness, its fearlessness, it is one of the finest human documents I know." It is alive with the breath of warm affection and calm courage. One sentence is all we need quote to show that, like so many others before and since, he had no fear of death. He wrote: "I tread the common road into the great darkness, without any thought of fear, and with very much of hope."

When that brave explorer, Robert Falcon Scott, lay waiting for death in the little tent on the deserted, snow-swept ice-field, he wrote with his frost-bitten fingers many messages to his friends, that prove with what supreme courage he met his end. A few words are enough to show his dauntless spirit: "The Great God has called me . . . but take comfort in that I die at peace with the world and myself . . . not afraid."

In death, as Isaac Disraeli has said, "The habitual associations of the natural character are most likely to prevail." Thus, Rabelais, who lived a cynic, died with a cynicism upon his lips: "I am going to seek a great perhaps"; while Cecil Rhodes, enthusiast and empire-builder, was heard on his death-bed to repeat the words of Tennyson,

"So much to do: so little done,"

and Dr. Adam, for many years headmaster of the Royal High School in Edinburgh, where Sir Walter Scott was one of his pupils, ended his life with the words, "You may go, boys! It is growing dark."

It falls to the lot of most doctors to see much of death, and I have watched by the bedside of the dying of many classes and of all ages. I have seen the little silken thread on which a child's life hung—a life so far as one could tell of infinite potentialities for good—snap suddenly, leaving only a terrible sense of the mystery and inscrutableness of it all; and I have fought with death, and lost the battle, over the beds of young men and women in the first flush of maturity; I have seen strong men and women cut down in their prime; I have watched the old totter down the slope into the twilight, and at the end fall asleep like little children, and I say it with a due sense of the importance of the statement, that my experience has been that, however much men and women may, when in the full vigour of health, fear death, when their hour approaches the fear is almost invariably lulled into quietness, and they face the end with calmness and a serene mind.

A man caught in the toils of severe but not mortal pain will sometimes gasp out the trembling question, "Am I dying?" But I cannot remember ever having been asked this question precisely in these words by anyone who was rapidly approaching that

"Undiscovered country from whose bourne
No traveller returns."

Most dying persons, with the exception of patients suffering from consumption, are aware that they are dying. They need no human tongue to tell them; they know intuitively, but they tend to keep the knowledge to themselves. Sometimes a man who is critically ill, who is, in fact, dying, will ask the question, not, "Am I going to die?" but couched in other language, though with the same essential meaning, "Am I going to get better?" And while one hesitates, to choose the kindliest word with which to make reply, the sick man will often add, "I am not afraid to know the truth."

The well known *spes phthisica* or "consumptives' hope" is an interesting manifestation of the psychology of the sick. Many patients dying of consumption manifest a cheery optimism that is often most reassuring for the relatives, and sometimes a little disconcerting for the physician, who knows that the patient's statements as to his sense of well-being are harshly contradicted by the physical signs of his disease. A consumptive patient, after the disease reaches a certain stage, is always "feeling better," and looks forward eagerly to the day when he will be able to resume his former occupation. He rarely believes that he is dying, and I have been assured by a young man a few hours before his death, and so weak that he could hardly whisper, that he would be all right in a month or two, when the warmer weather should come.

A medical friend who has an extensive experience of consumptive patients in a large workhouse hospital, tells me that in a ward in which there are many patients in advanced stages of the disease, and among whom a death is a very frequent occurrence, the survivors treat these catastrophes with a stolid nonchalance. Apparently each appropriates for himself the gratifying belief that he is immune to the common lot which is overwhelming his companions. They may all die, he is "feeling better." Nowhere does Young's line, "All men think all men mortal but themselves," find a more illuminating commentary than in a ward of consumptive patients.

Every doctor has known men and women, whom their intimates would never have regarded as being cast in any particularly heroic mould, evince a wonderful self-control when confronted suddenly, as not infrequently happens, with two weighty alternatives, viz., the prospect of an immediate serious operation from which they may not recover, and the certain alternative of death. Very often, in such circumstances, the patient has been calmer than the calmest of his friends, and has come to a decision with a clear judgment, and with no sign of fear.

Even in the most timid men and women there would seem to be a hidden reserve of courage stored up against emergencies, and it is when he is faced by the big things of life that the best that is in a man is drawn to the surface.

Some years ago I made the acquaintance of a nurse who, a few months before, in the midst of her work had been seized by a formidable complication, viz., the perforation of a gastric ulcer from which she suffered. Her surgical experience had taught her that her condition was one of jeopardy, and she knew that, though an operation might save her, death stared her in the face. The operation was performed successfully, and she recovered. I asked her whether, in the shadow of imminent death, she had felt any fear, and her answer was, "No, I have a natural human shrinking from death when in perfect health, but when on the edge of the precipice I had absolutely no fear."

Those who meet death suddenly by accident, in all probability are not "surprised of fear." A young man who fell from the roof of a lofty building and escaped, miraculously, with a handful of bruises, assured me that, in his long fall to earth, which seemed to cover an eternity, he did not feel the slightest fear; and I have been told by three medical men, each of whom narrowly escaped drowning under entirely different circumstances, that when their fate seemed certain all fear was taken from them. One of them tells me that at the moment of his greatest danger he felt quite unconcerned, and did not experience the slightest anxiety until he was about to be rescued, when he was unexpectedly assailed by a timorous wonder as to whether the rescue-boat would reach him in time. So long as he had no hope of safety, he had no fear. Another assures me that the alarm which attended his discovery that he was being swept away powerless before the tide rapidly gave place, as his strength became exhausted, to a comfortable condition of indifference, and his last thought before he lost consciousness was one of quiet amusement. He saw a fussy but futile gentleman dash frantically from the beach into the sea, with heroic but indeterminate intentions of bringing succour, and, after thoroughly wetting himself, retire hastily to the beach again. This was the last thing he remembers seeing before unconsciousness supervened, and the sight provoked him to the thought, "What a funny thing to do."

Dr. Livingstone, seized and mauled by a lion, felt neither pain nor fear, and from his experience ventured to suggest that a kindly Providence mitigates in like fashion the suffering of animals when they fall a prey to the carnivora. On one occasion he jocularly informed an interviewer that, when in the lion's clutches, his only thought was which part of him the beast would devour first.

That most delightful essayist, Mr. A. C. Benson, puts on record in "Along the Road" his personal experience when face to face with death. When climbing in the Alps he fell over the edge of a crevasse, and for a period of twenty minutes there was nothing between him and death but the strands of a frail rope and the devotion of his friend and a guide. He says: "Suddenly it dawned upon me that I was doomed. . . . The strange thing was that I had no sense of fear, only a dim wonder as to how I should die, and whether the fall would kill me at once. I had no edifying thoughts. I did not review my past life or my many failings. I wondered that a second fatal accident should happen so soon at the same place, thought a little of my relatives, and of Eton where I was a master, wondered who would succeed to my boarding-house, and how my pupils would be arranged for. I remember, too, speculating what death would be like. . . . Then I think I did become unconscious for a moment, my last thought being a sort of anxious longing to get the thing over as soon as possible."

Fortunately for the literature of our time he was saved by the magnificent bravery of the guide and his companion, and in summing up the matter, he says: "The time had not seemed at all long to me; and, as I have said, I had no touch of pain, only faintness and discomfort, and no sense either of dread or fear."

Our third source of evidence for the statement that the dying do not fear death is the testimony of those who have been by many death-beds. Personally, I have never seen anyone about to die evince the slightest fear of the impending change, and this experience is supported by a great body of weighty medical opinion. Sir Benjamin Brodie who, a century ago, was the acknowledged *doyen* of surgery in England, has left the following record in one of his conversational essays: "I have myself never known but two instances in which, in the act of dying, there were manifest indications of the fear of death. The individuals to whom I allude were unexpectedly destroyed by hæmorrhage, which, from peculiar circumstances, which I need not now explain, it was impossible to suppress." Brodie was a man of very wide experience which ranged through every social grade from Windsor Castle to the slums of

London, and in his day he must have seen many people die. But only two, an infinitesimal proportion of the whole, showed fear.

That men and women can school themselves to face, without flinching, the steady approach of inevitable death is proved from the conduct of many sufferers from incurable disease who know that their days are numbered. At the present moment I know three sufferers from cancer, inoperable and incurable, for whom all that can be done has been done without avail. Each knows that the final stage of the journey has been entered upon; but each preserves a calm and untroubled mind, and is ready to face the end whenever it may come. One, a woman, is buoyed up by a confident religious faith, and she looks forward to death as

"Only a step into the open air
Out of a tent already luminous
With light that shines through its transparent walls."

The other two are men, who find consolation in a rough-hewn philosophy of their own. They believe, with Montaigne, that "Death is a part of the constitution of the universe; it is a part of the life of the world."

The late Sir J. F. Goodhart, one of the most eminent of London's consulting physicians, and an authority of world-wide renown upon the diseases of children, when a resident doctor in Guy's Hospital arranged with the sister in charge of his wards that he should be called to every patient who seemed to be dying. "I wanted," he says, "apart from my duties, to obtain also some actual knowledge of facts that foretell immediate dissolution." And out of those trying experiences he gathered these grains of comfort: "I am never tired of saying, because I am sure it is as true as it is comforting, although in opposition to the general belief, that death has no terror for the sick man," and also this: "There is nothing terrible to the dying in death itself. The veil between two worlds is but a cloud, and one passes through it imperceptibly."

Sir William Osler, scholarly humanist and erudite physician, has placed his opinion on record in the following words: "I have careful notes of about five hundred deathbeds, studied particularly with reference to the modes of death and the sensations of the dying. Ninety suffered bodily pain or distress of one sort or another; eleven showed mental apprehension; two positive terror; one expressed spiritual exaltation; one bitter remorse. The great majority gave no sign one way or the other; like their birth, their death was a sleep and a forgetting."

Criminal psychology is an interesting study, and although one shrinks from making any general deductions from the conduct of murderers about to suffer capital punishment, their bearing in the last few moments of life is instructive.

Some behave with a bovine indifference; others make a mighty show of bravado; and others again manifest a curious interest in the lesser affairs of the world which they are soon about to leave. I cannot vouch for the truth of the following incident, which I find in Alexander Smith's exquisite essay, *A Lark's Flight*, but equally remarkable displays of insouciance have been made upon the scaffold:

"It is said that the championship of England was to be decided at some little distance from London on the morning of the day on which Thurtell was executed, and that, when he came out on the scaffold, he inquired privily of the executioner if the result had yet become known. Jack Ketch was not aware, and Thurtell expressed his regret that the ceremony in which he was the chief actor should take place so inconveniently early in the day."

There is more than a gleam of pawky humour in the incident recounted by Sir Melville L. MacNaghten in his book of reminiscences. Fowler and Millsom, the

Muswell Hill murderers, were executed together; but as Fowler, in the dock, had made a violent attempt to get at Millsom, who had turned Queen's evidence, they were kept apart upon the scaffold, and a man, Seaman, who was to be executed with them, was placed on the trap-door between them. At this, the penultimate moment of his life, a quaint conceit would seem to have been born in the mind of Seaman, who was heard to say: "This is the first time as ever I was a —— peacemaker." The words prove that all his faculties were alive; but he was obviously, as Sir Melville suggests, "insensible of mortality."

Mr. Thomas Holmes, Secretary of the Howard Association, and author of *Known to the Police*, is thoroughly acquainted with the mind of the criminal in its many phases, and he has procured much valuable information as to the conduct and character of murderers. On one occasion he asked the chaplain of a large prison to tell him whether sorrow, remorse, or fear were ever shown by men about to pay the penalty for a premeditated murder. The chaplain's reply was "that he had performed his last sad offices for a considerable number of such prisoners, and he had discovered neither fear nor remorse in any of them."

A prison doctor who has had a large experience of judicial executions informs me that he has never seen a criminal on his way to the scaffold betray any outward evidence of fear. This fact he attributes in a large measure to the careful but painful ministrations of the prison chaplains, to whose work he paid a well-merited tribute of praise.

We must draw a line of sharp distinction between the fear of death, and reluctance to die. The latter is often the outcome of a torturing anxiety as to the welfare and future happiness of those who are about to be left behind. When the father of a family is cut down by a mortal disease in the midtime of his days, his last moments are often harassed, not by the fear of death itself, but by a nameless dread that his demise may mean hardship, distress, and possibly poverty for his widow and children, for whom he has been unable to make adequate provision. I remember attending a young man, married for barely a year, who died from heart-failure supervening on pneumonia. A few hours before the end came he realized that he was dying, and his distress of mind was most poignant. His wife was expecting soon to become a mother, and his one thought was of her. His faint but constantly repeated cry was, "My little girl. What will my little girl do?" But when a solemn promise had been given that his wife and unborn child would be taken care of and provided for, his distress melted into a great calm, and he sank into unconsciousness, which gradually deepened into death, comforted and unafraid.

It was a similar hideous anxiety that, more than Antarctic cold and the pangs of hunger, darkened the last brave hours of

Captain Scott. In the many letters he wrote during the last few days of life with his dying or dead companions stretched in the little tent beside him, there were no words either of complaint or fear; but over and over again there was the cry that those dependent upon himself and his fellow-sufferers, should not be left desolate. Indeed the very last entry which his dying fingers wrote was:

"For God's sake, look after our people."

Any doctor who has had much experience of hospital practice will readily pay a tribute of admiration to that large body of people, who, by an unwarrantable limitation of the term, are known as the working classes. Their patience in sickness is extraordinary, and is often a reproach to those who are more fortunately situated, while their bravery is beyond all praise. A man who has been mangled by machinery, or been bruised and battered out of all semblance to a human being by some terrible explosion—a clod of common clay—will show a brave and undaunted heart when called to face the unknown mysteries of a formidable operation, or when he can hear about his bed "The wind of Death's imperishable wing." And the working woman in like case is no less brave. For herself she has no fear, but her heart is sore for her little ones; and if some kindly nurse wins her confidence she will confess that her tears are not the expression of any pity or anxiety for herself, but are wrung out of her heart when she wonders what is to become of her children when their mother is taken from them. We are, here, face to face with one of the things that make it hard to die. It is the parting from objects or persons that hold a large place in our affections; for the ties of human love are too exquisitely tender to be harshly torn asunder without provoking acute pain. Dr. Johnson, with a wonderful insight into the human heart, spoke no more than the truth when he said to his old pupil Garrick, who had been showing him his possessions, and the beauty of his new home at Hampton, "Ah! David, David, it is things like these that make a death-bed terrible."

It was not the fear of death, but simply reluctance to die, that forced from the lips of Charlotte Brontë, whose ears had caught some whispered petition that God would spare her, the pathetic cry, "Oh! I am not going to die, am I? He will not separate us, we have been so happy."

But it was the numbing sense of pain at the thought that the few, brief, happy months, in a life that all along had been lived in the atmosphere of tragedy, were to come to an end, and the dawning of the knowledge that she must part from the husband for whom she had waited so patiently, and not live to know the joys of motherhood of which she had dreamed, that wrung this cry from her heart.

CHAPTER V
THE PAINLESSNESS OF DEATH

" 'Αναίσθητον ὁ θάνατος."

DIOGENES THE EPICUREAN.

"If I had strength enough to hold a pen I would write down how easy and pleasant a thing it is to die."

DR. WILLIAM HUNTER (his last words).

"In death itself there can be nothing terrible, for the act of death annihilates sensation."

COLTON.

CHAPTER V

THE PAINLESSNESS OF DEATH

Is it a painful thing to die? This is a question which, unuttered, must have passed through the minds of all who have ever given a thought to death. In all likelihood there is as little pain in the act of death as there is in falling asleep. In considering this matter we must be careful to limit our issue. We are not discussing whether disease is attended by pain for the individual, or whether the death of some dear one provokes pain in the hearts of the bereaved. We wish to ascertain, as nearly as we can, whether death, the cessation of vitality, is a painful process.

If there were more "compulsory Greek" there would be a truer appreciation of the word values of the English language. The phrase "death-agony" has brought much confusion into this matter. It suggests pain of an acute character, though, really, it means nothing of the sort.

Death "agony" is simply the final struggle or conflict of the forces of life against the overmastering power that is about to extinguish them. It is the last guttering or flickering of the candle before it goes out.

It is probable that in most cases a dying person is unconscious of the final stages of his disease, and that the laboured breathing, which is so distressing for the onlooker, or the convulsive struggles seen in certain diseases, do not betoken any suffering on the part of the patient.

One has sometimes seen a healthy individual lying on his back in a profound sleep, breathing with great effort, with much stertor, and with every appearance of distress. He is, apparently, being slowly asphyxiated. His tongue has fallen back and obstructed the orifice of the windpipe, and respiration can only be conducted with great difficulty. But if one turn such a person on his side, and draw the tongue gently forward, the breathing immediately becomes easy; and if one wake the sleeper to ask if he were conscious of any distress during his slumber, he is certain to say "No!" I have seen healthy sleepers apparently suffer more than the dying, and know nothing whatever about it.

In February, 1914, an interesting correspondence took place in the columns of the *Times* as to whether the act of death is associated with physical pain. Much interesting evidence was offered from many quarters, but I shall make use of only two of the letters published. One was from Professor J. Cook Wilson, who described the terrible respiratory struggles of his father, when dying from cardiac failure supervening on influenza. The harrowing struggles of the dying man were apparently so painful that his son could hardly believe the assurance of the medical attendants that the patient knew nothing of them. After several hours passed, apparently, in intense agony the patient woke up, and volunteered the statement that he had spent a comfortable night. This was unexpected but very gratifying corroboration of the physician's opinion. Another correspondent contributed a personal experience. He had narrowly escaped death from typhoid fever in a mining camp in Mexico, and after his recovery he was informed by his friends that in his delirium he had shrieked and fought as though suffering untold agonies. As a matter of fact he had, all the while, been entirely free from pain, anxiety, or fear.

It is a painful thing to witness an epileptic convulsion, and these convulsions may sometimes be so violent that muscles are ruptured or torn from their attachments. Yet, the sufferer, when the fit is over, has absolutely no knowledge of the terrible convulsion through which he has passed, and is at a loss to explain how he has bitten his tongue or torn his muscle.

I have never seen anyone in the throes of death present such an appearance of intense and violent suffering as I have seen patients manifest in the convulsions of eclampsia and uræmia. Eclampsia is a formidable complication that is sometimes met with at child-birth, and varies considerably in intensity. The convulsions may be prolonged and very severe, and the patient would appear to be suffering unspeakable torture. Sometimes the muscles of the face are distorted into the mask of acute agony, but, when the convulsion is over, the patient is quite unaware of what she has passed through. One of the worst cases of eclamptic convulsion I ever saw, occurred in a woman aged twenty-eight. I was present at the moment of onset, and saw agony graven in sharp characters upon the sufferer's face. But when the convulsion was over the patient slowly recovered consciousness and, as she opened her eyes, said, "I have had a nice little sleep."

Uræmic convulsions, which sometimes supervene on Bright's disease, are also, apparently, attended by acute pain; but the patient is perfectly unconscious of them. In all likelihood this holds true of the dying. The sensorium is blunted by disease, and by the accumulation of poisons in the circulating blood, and the symptoms that are so painful for the healthy observer to witness have often no meaning for the person who is manifesting them.

Some diseases that terminate fatally are undoubtedly attended by much pain; but we are not justified in transferring to death, which puts an end to the sufferings, the responsibility for the distress which may precede it. The sufferings are the result of disease; they are in no sense a part of death. On the other hand there are many diseases which are attended by little physical pain. I have been assured by a patient, a few days before his death, that in a long illness of several months' duration he had suffered no pain, but only a little discomfort. So we may reach the gate of death without passing through any avenue of pain upon our way.

We can never have definite first-hand knowledge as to whether the final act, the very act of death, is painful. The dead man knows the secret, but an eternal silence lies upon his lips, and he cannot tell us. We can, however, get very near the point. Persons who have been rescued from death by drowning, and been restored to consciousness only after many hours of careful treatment, testify that at the moment of immersion and before consciousness began to fail they suffered much distress. But, by and by, the distress gave place to a feeling of drowsy comfort in which they remained until consciousness was completely lost. Some of them go the length of saying that it is much more painful to be resuscitated than to drown.

In his *Psychological Inquiries* Sir Benjamin Brodie quotes the case of a sailor who, after his rescue from the sea, lay for a long time insensible. On recovering consciousness he declared that "he had been in heaven, and complained bitterly of his being restored to life as a great hardship."

In his *Historia Vitæ et Mortis*, Bacon records the following incident. A young man, anxious to know what the feelings of those who hanged themselves might be, made a personal experiment. After he had been cut down and resuscitated he was asked what he had suffered, and he replied that he had felt no pain. ("*Ille interrogatus quid passus esset, retulit se dolorem non sensisse.*")

The poet Cowper, who made at least three attempts to escape from the melancholy obsessions that from time to time rendered his life a misery, has put it on record that when he tried to commit suicide by hanging in his room in the Temple he experienced no pain.

Sir Francis Younghusband, that distinguished soldier who was the first to lead a British force to the forbidden capital of Thibet, was almost killed, a few years ago, by a motor-car which ran him down. He has enshrined his experiences in the delightful little book *Within*, which was the fruit of his convalescence. He says: "Then came the crash. I seemed to be whirling in a wild struggle with the machine. Was it to be death? It seemed it must be. And if death had resulted it would have been absolutely painless, for no pain had yet come. There would have been simply extinction, without suffering and without thought. I would just have been obliterated like a moth in the candle or the caterpillar beneath our feet, and suffered as little. In an instant the full current of life, with all its unfulfilled purposes, and ties of love and affection, would have been brought to a stop. But I myself would have felt as little as an electric lamp when the current is switched off. The light would have gone out, but there would have been no pain."

Tyndall, who was once rendered unconscious by an electric shock, believed that death by lightning stroke must be painless.

We begin our lives unconsciously. Not one of us has any memory of that sublime moment in our history when we first began to exist, or, as Tennyson has put it:

> '. . . Star and system rolling past
> A soul shall draw from out the vast,
> And strike his being into bounds."

We are equally unconscious of having suffered any pain at the moment of our birth. The pangs of birth are the mother's; the child, in all likelihood, does not suffer during its entry into the world, for its delicate organization could not survive such an ordeal. And so it is not unlikely that when the end comes, and we throw off life like a garment, we shall feel no pain.

That fascinating and courtly physician,

Sir William Gull, who, in his long experience at Guy's Hospital and in private, must have stood by many death-beds, is said to have comforted a querulous old gentleman, who feared that death might be a painful act, with the words, "My dear sir, you will know nothing about it, it will be just as easy as being born."

In curious contrast with those who believe that it is a painful thing to die, we have the opinion of Sir James Paget, the eminent surgeon, who was inclined to think that if we were conscious of the act of death we might discover it to be a pleasurable sensation. This idea finds confirmation in the words of William Hunter, the great anatomist and surgeon, who, with his dying breath, whispered to a friend: "If I had strength enough to hold a pen I would write down how easy and pleasant a thing it is to die."

Those who have seen much of death are agreed that it is often a difficult matter to determine the precise moment at which the final change occurs, so imperceptibly and quietly does life merge into death. There is no physician who has not stood, many a time, in a hushed room, with a finger on a flickering pulse and watched the end supervene so gently that not till he had placed his stethoscope over the heart could he be sure that "Life's fitful fever" was over. This is how the great change usually supervenes in old people—a gradual somnolence, passing by gradations into a deeper and deeper slumber till, as the ancient Greek philosopher Diogenes of Sinope said, "One brother begins to embrace the other," and sleep is swallowed up in death. In most cases they

"Drift on through slumber to a dream
and through a dream to death."

The death of a child is often as imperceptible, and at any age the end may occur so quietly as to be almost unobserved. The poet Hood showed himself to be an excellent clinical observer when he wrote:

"We thought her dying while she slept,
And sleeping when she died."

These facts are opposed to the idea that death is a process attended by pain. They indicate, on the other hand, that whatever may have been the sufferings of the patient in his last illness, the moment of death is free from all distress. We cannot conceive that pain is a necessary and inseparable attribute of death when we remember how many people pass away so suddenly and imperceptibly that their companions fail to notice that they have died. A husband and wife retire to rest at night apparently in perfect health. In the silent watches the long finger of death is laid upon one of them, and the end comes so quietly that the other sleeper is not disturbed. Some years ago I was called to see an old lady who had died in her easy-chair at the fireside. She had been reading a book, which her daughter, who was sewing in the same room, heard fall upon the floor. She imagined that her mother had gone to sleep, and gently lowered the light that her sleep might not be interrupted. But it was a sleep that nothing could disturb: it was the sleep of death.

A busy city man falls in a heap, dead, after writing a cablegram; another apparently faints in the train or the tram without sign or symptom of distress; another opens his door in the morning and drops dead on the threshold, all without a cry. There can be no agony in such deaths as these, and such deaths are daily occurrences. Not a few doctors pass over in silence the petition in the Litany which asks for deliverance from sudden death. For they believe that to die in the twinkling of an eye is better than to come to the crossing after long months of sickness.[1]

In character, temperament, and religious belief John Milton and Alexander Pope

---

[1] I have it on high ecclesiastical authority that this is a misinterpretation of the Litany. "Sudden death," I am informed, means death in an unprepared state.

were wide as the poles asunder. But there was a remarkable similarity in the manner of their death. Milton, our great organ-voiced Puritan, afflicted with blindness for years and a martyr to gout in its most painful form, died, as Johnson puts it, "by a quiet and silent expiration about the tenth of November, 1674, at his house in Bunhill-Fields."

Pope had been a sufferer from physical defects all his days, and during the concluding five years of his life he was a martyr to asthma and other distressing maladies for which the medical science of the day could offer him little, if any, relief. The month of May, 1744, was one of much physical and mental distress for him. At times he was delirious, and again he had delusions and hallucinations. But, "He died in the evening of the thirtieth day of May, 1744, so placidly that the attendants did not discern the exact time of his expiration."

The gentle fashion in which death comes

to the aged is well illustrated by the closing hours of the Wesleys. From his student days at Oxford, where he injured his health by overstudy, Charles Wesley, who bequeathed to the literature of hymnology some of the sweetest lyrics that inspired pen ever indited, had been a confirmed hypochondriac. As Southey says, "He had always dreaded the act of dying, and his prayer was that God would grant him patience and an easy death. A calmer frame of mind and an easier passage could not have been granted him; the powers of life were fairly worn out, and without any disease, he fell asleep." This was in his eightieth year. Three years later, at the age of 88, "in sure and certain hope of Eternal Life," John Wesley laid his armour down. Some months before he died he wrote: "I am now an old man, decayed from head to foot. My eyes are dim, my right hand shakes much; my mouth is hot and dry every morning; I have a lingering fever almost every day; my motion is weak and slow." A little later he wrote: "I feel no pain from head to foot; only, it seems, nature is exhausted, and, humanly speaking, will sink more and more till

"The weary springs of life stand still at last."

He died on the second day of March, 1791, after a few days of weakness and increasing lethargy, passing "peacefully away about ten o'clock."

"His face was placid, and the expression which death had fixed upon his venerable features was that of a serene and heavenly smile." In describing his closing years Southey says, "Other persons perceived his growing weakness before he was thus aware of it himself; the most marked symptom was that of a frequent disposition to sleep during the day . . . the involuntary slumbers which came upon him in the latter years of his life were indications that the machine was wearing out, and would soon come to a stop."

So death came to them, and to myriads of others of the sons of men, not as a torturer bringing untold agony, but as an angel of sleep:

"And so, when life's sweet Fable ends,
 The soul and body part, like friends."

There is no "agony" in death, whatever may have been the nature of the sickness which has preceded it. Death is like the restful calm that falls upon the sea after the tumult of a wild storm.

CHAPTER VI
EUTHANASIA

"Bis est mori alterius arbitrio mori."

PUBLIUS LOCHIUS SYRUS.

"Darkling I listen; and, for many a time
  I have been half in love with easeful death,
Call'd him soft names in many a musèd rhyme,
  To take into the air my quiet breath;
Now more than ever seems it rich to die,
  To cease upon the midnight with no pain,
While thou art pouring forth thy soul abroad
  In such an ecstasy!"

JOHN KEATS.

CHAPTER VI

EUTHANASIA

WE have already seen that in all likelihood the act of death is free from pain; but we must admit that some of the illnesses which terminate in death are accompanied by much suffering. The suffering may be very severe, as in cases of angina pectoris, meningitis, peritonitis, tetanus, or cancer affecting certain regions of the body. In angina pectoris the agony is intense, but it is spasmodic and not continuous, and if, as all too frequently is the case, the spasm culminate in death, the act of death must come as a pleasurable relief.

In meningitis the most painful stage is the preliminary one, when every loud sound or ray of light sends an arrow of fire through the tortured brain. But once the disease is established the sufferer drifts into a condition of unconsciousness which usually persists for several days, and terminates in death.

In peritonitis the pain is very acute, and is increased by the pressure of the lightest covering. But in most cases of peritonitis, if at all extensive, there is a rapid absorption of poisonous substances which rapidly brings about unconsciousness, and the patient no longer feels.

In tetanus, or lock-jaw, we are dealing with an affection which is characterized by severe convulsions, during which the patient does not lose consciousness. It shares this evil peculiarity with hydrophobia. In practically every other disease attended with convulsions, consciousness is lost during the fit. But it is otherwise with tetanus and hydrophobia, the sufferers from which are hideously aware of the torture they are enduring. We can imagine with what relief the "agony" of death will be hailed by such sufferers.

Cancer is not necessarily a painful disease, but it can produce unspeakable torture if any sensory nerve become involved. Science has done much to mitigate the suffering inseparable from these affections, and most physicians must many times have endorsed John Hunter's fervent exclamation, "Thank God for opium." Opium is only one of a large number of pain-subduing remedies which are now at our disposal, and a wise physician knows when to make use of them. But they should never be abused.

Many times I have discussed the question whether, in a hopeless case attended by much suffering, the physician would be justified in giving a lethal dose of morphia to his patient. As a rule the layman argues strongly that this should be done. But the responsibility is not on his shoulders, and, if it were, his conclusion would not come so glibly from his lips. It is always an easy thing to solve, in the abstract, a difficulty with which we are never likely to be faced. This makes it a light matter for a philosopher and poet like Maeterlinck to look forward to a time when medical science will mercifully put all incurables to death.

Expressed in its simplest terms, the supreme objection to this procedure is that we cannot give life, so we have no right to take it. In spite of all her miracles, Science has not yet succeeded in creating so elementary a thing as a blade of living grass: she cannot breathe the breath of life into the bones of the dead. She has, therefore, no right to hurry and hustle a living being across the threshold of eternity. *Litera scripta manet*—"Thou shalt not kill."

We must never forget that human judgment is not infallible, and many a sick person who has been given up by the most capable physicians has recovered. The following case is quoted on the authority of the *Journal of the American Medical Association.* Some years ago a clergyman's wife, who was believed to be suffering from a hopeless malady, published, in various newspapers throughout the United States, a letter in which she urged upon the medical profession the advisability of showing her "scientific kindness" which would bring her sufferings to an end and give her a painless death. "She received many replies endorsing her argument that physicians should be permitted to put her and other similarly unfortunate patients out of their misery. Apparently, however, the lady is to-day glad that her plea did not prevail, as she is reported to have been completely restored to health by a surgical operation, and to be perfectly well."

If it were an accepted rule of medical practice that a suffering sick person, if deemed past human aid in the opinion of two or more medical men, could at his own request, or on the request of his relatives, be hustled gently but firmly through the gate of death, the way would be open to all manner of abuse. The life of a doctor is already beset by more than enough anxieties, and if to his other burdens were added this final decision—if the law of the land and the opinion of the people, which do not always coincide, were agreed upon this matter, I am firmly convinced that the medical profession would decline the responsibility. Medicine is, and ought to be, the art of healing, not of dealing death, and no doctor would willingly consent to carry an executioner's death-warrant in his pocket.

I have heard perfectly sane and reasonable people say that all sufferers from cancer should be mercifully put to death. To express such an opinion is, at the lowest, to be guilty of gross moral cowardice. We are becoming so emasculate that the very idea of pain makes us flee to extremes of action. In itself pain is not necessarily an evil, and, although hard to bear, it is often beneficent and may even come as an angel in disguise. Moreover, we must never forget that though the death-roll from cancerous disease is enormously large, and though the most patient researches of brilliant investigators have as yet given us no clue either to the cause or the certain cure of the affection, not a few cases are cured by operation, some have been healed by the X-rays and by radium, while some few cases are said to have undergone spontaneous cure. I have sometimes wondered whether the calmly expressed views of these dogmatic theorists would withstand the shock of a personal experience, and whether one of them, found to be suffering from cancer or an incurable form of heart-disease, would come and ask me to help him to translate his frequently expressed opinion into a lethal fact. One man in a thousand might; but the cup of life is so sweet for most of us that, even though the dregs may be bitter and scald like liquid fire, few men will lay it willingly down before the last drop is drained. The duty of the physician is to assuage the more intolerable pain of his patient by the judicious use of those anodynes with which science has supplied him, and to render what of life remains to him as comfortable as possible; but he must not constitute himself the arbiter of another's right to live.

When we examine closely the popular attitude towards this matter we find that it is nothing more or less than the affirmation of an unconfessed and probably unrecognized selfishness. How often one hears the friend of a dying person say: "I wish it were all over, I cannot bear to see him suffer." Now this expression, which every doctor has heard a hundred times, is not the outcome of true affection, but is the bastard thought of a weak and selfish nature. The personal pronoun is the chief weight in the scale. "*I* cannot bear," therefore he whom I called friend may hasten with his dying.

Civilization and luxury have made us such otiose creatures that we hate and shrink from the little inconveniences, the unpleasantness for ourselves, the suspense, the anxiety, and the emotional strain which the last illness of a friend involves us in. It is not the suffering of the patient, which applied medical skill is probably alleviating, but our own intolerance of personal distress which makes us shrink from the death-bed of a friend.

The care of the dying is one of the most delicate offices of the physician. Much may be done, in a thousand little ways, to make the last stages of the journey easier for the traveller. The arrangement of the pillows, the weight of the bed-clothes, the position of the body, the timely administration of nourishment, the gentle prevision that anticipates the wishes which the failing mind can hardly formulate, and the many artifices of kindness with which a good nurse surrounds a death-bed all help to make the traveller's passing easier, alike for traveller and friend.

Though it is his duty to fight death every inch of the way, a wise physician will know when to cease from administering powerful stimulants such as strychnine and digitalin, strong tonics for the nervous system and heart. Up to a certain point they are invaluable in lengthening life, but when that point is reached the physician should lay them down. Thereafter their use does not prolong life; it only slows down the approach of death.

CHAPTER VII
WHAT LIFE GAINS FROM DEATH

"You never know what life means till you die.
Even throughout life, 'tis death that makes life live,
Gives it whatever the significance."

        ROBERT BROWNING.

"If life did not end, if it were a process of infinite duration, it would be devoid of the precious things that make us yearn for its everlasting perpetuation."

        CASSIUS J. KEYSER.

CHAPTER VII

WHAT LIFE GAINS FROM DEATH

WE are so accustomed to regard death from such wrong angles and in such defective light that we often fail to see the many benefits it confers on life. Tradition has taught us to look upon death as an inevitable evil. True vision will show us that, without death, life would lose many of its subtler beauties.

Our mortality is a provision necessary for the transmission of life. If there were no death, neither you who read these words nor I who write them would ever have walked this earth; for long before we were ushered into life the world would have been filled to overflowing with a jostling crowd of human beings, cursed with the gift of physical immortality, and there would have been no elbow room for more. Death makes possible the transference of life, with all its opportunities, from one generation to another:

"Et quasi cursores vitai lampada tradunt."

And death gives life dynamic. If man knew that his days on earth were to be endless, if he were conscious that he would still persist, through infinite æons of time, with the same body and the same faculties as he has to-day, a denizen of the same earth, all incentive to bestir himself except to seek food and clothing would be lost. There would be no desire to make his mark in the world; no stimulating ambition to leave the world a little better than he found it; no hungry aspiration to be remembered after he is dead —for death is not to lay hands upon him. If there were no death, life would become a thing stagnant, monotonous and unspeakably burdensome.

Practically all the progress that man has made is due to the fact that he is mortal.

How Death Enriches Life

He has recognized that he is in this world only for a little while, and this knowledge has been a goad to stimulate him to make diligent use of whatever talents he is endowed with. The secrets of Nature have been wrested from her grudging fingers by men who, knowing they were mortal, have sought to comprehend the mysteries of the world around them in the hope that knowledge might enable them, if not to circumvent death, at least to ameliorate the asperities of life for themselves and others. The consciousness of his finite life has compelled man to overcome his natural inertia, with the result that he ceases to live an entirely vegetative existence.

Every event of our lives is coloured and conditioned by our mortality. Death gives to each of them a new value, and we focus the facts of life more sharply because they are hedged about by death.

All our instincts and emotions are reinforced by death. If we were not mortal, the paternal and the maternal instincts would not dominate our lives so strongly as they do. If we knew that we should never die, we should have no desire for children to perpetuate our names and carry on the succession of the race. If we were not mortal, children would be regarded as a superfluous encumbrance: unnecessary and unwelcome occupiers of earth-space already sufficiently limited; impudent little interlopers for whom the world has no need. Thus, ultimately, we should arrive at a world without a child, surely a drearier and more desolate world than the blackest inferno ever conjured up by the morbid imagination of some self-torturing anchorite of the middle ages.

A world without a child would be a place in which there was no call for some of the finer and most beautiful emotions to which the human soul can give expression. If we were robbed of the opportunity of lavishing our affection on little children our natures would run the risk of becoming warped and atrophied.

As George Eliot said, "In every parting there is an image of death," and it is this simulacrum which flavours all human farewells with a sweet sadness, while it hallows all reunions with a holy joy. When a mother parts with her first-born son, whom the adventure of life has called to the other end of the world, it is death that gives a special poignancy to their parting. They may never see each other on earth again. That is the unspoken thought, that, like a drawn sword, lies keen upon their hearts, and it is that which gives a fragrance to every letter that passes between them during the long years of their separation, and which makes holy ground of the old hearth-stone when they foregather about it again.

And death lends a peculiar sanctity to human love. Is not the marriage promise, "till death us do part?" The bride of a man's youth, the faithful counsellor of his middle life, and the loyal companion of his old age is made dearer to him, and he to her, by the knowledge that some day death will separate them. And it is the same knowledge that makes a young mother clasp her sick child to her breast in an impotent agony of love and fear. A man may love his books, he may be proud of his collection of pictures, of old furniture, or of ancient brasses, but the love he bears his wife, his children, or his friends is something deeper and more sublime; it is a love intensified and purified by the thought that human life is a finite thing, which may at any moment be touched by the finger of death.

In the moulding of the history of mankind, death has played a supreme part. Without death human progress would have been infinitely slower than it has been, and the onrush of civilization would have been stayed by ancient tyrants and their tyrannies. If Nero or Caligula had been physically immortal the amount of human suffering would have been incalculably increased. But their power for evil was cut short by the hand of death, which brings to an end both despot and slave. Death is a great liberator: it frees the individual from the trammels of life; but it also frees the race from the shackles of the past. All careful students of history, which, in the words of Gibbon, "is indeed little more than the register of the crimes, follies, and misfortunes of mankind," are fully persuaded of the ultimate triumph of right over wrong. It is a lesson that the poets have never wearied of teaching, as witness Longfellow's lines:

"Though the mills of God grind slowly, yet
    they grind exceeding small;
Though with patience He stands waiting, with
    exactness grinds He all."

or Bryant's:

"Truth crushed to earth shall rise again,
The eternal years of God are hers."

But the part played by death in the attainment of this result is too often lost sight of. It is not so much the effluxion of time, as the scavenging of death, which gives to the events of history the justice of true perspective. So long as the participators in some great accomplishment are still alive, it is almost impossible to estimate with accuracy the true value, the justice or injustice, of their deeds. They tend to preserve the atmosphere in which the event was consummated; they cannot rid themselves of the spirit of partisanship; their prejudices or biases persist with them, and tend to leaven the opinion of their contemporaries. But one by one they make their exit from the stage; the limelight is extinguished with them; the orchestra is silent, and the clean air of heaven sweeps the edifice ere the new players and the fresh spectators take their places. Then, and not till then, does it become possible to appraise at its true worth the performance of the departed players.

Under the directing finger of the great

First Cause man has climbed slowly, with bleeding feet and torn hands, from lower types to the development of to-day. If there had been no death, it is very doubtful if man would yet have attained his present degree of evolution. Death has rapidly suppressed the atypical, the weaklings, and those not qualified for survival; the "fittest" have been spared the longest, and whatever physical, or mental, or moral quality has had value, has tended to persist.

It is impossible to judge of the beauty and symmetry of some great building until the scaffolding which was a necessary accompaniment of its erection has been removed. Death clears away the scaffolding that has hedged about the growth of man, and we are what we are to-day, because death has helped to fashion us.

The psychological law of relativity teaches us that we know things only by their opposites. Without death we should be likely to hold life as of little account. Its very finite-ness gives life a special value, and a special beauty—the beauty of the evanescent. And many of the qualities that make us cling to life, are qualities that have been conferred upon it by death.

CHAPTER VIII

DOES DEATH END ALL?
(1) IS MAN MORE THAN MATTER?

"Your mental life is destitute of all the qualities of material existence, and it possesses all the qualities which the material existence lacks. Matter and mind belong to different realms. They are separated by the whole diameter of being."

Professor A. W. Momerie.

"Is it only a chance concourse of atoms, organized into a brain . . . from which comes the confident voice: I love, I hope, I worship eternal beauty, I offer myself in obedience to a perfect law of righteousness, I gladly suffer that others may be saved, I resist the threatening evil that I see? . . . Molecules, however organized, do not naturally thus utter themselves; chemical reactions are not thus expressed."

Samuel McChord Crothers.

"There is not room for Death,
Nor atom that his might could render void:
Thou, Thou art Being and Breath,
And what Thou art may never be destroyed."

Emily Brontë.

CHAPTER VIII

DOES DEATH END ALL? (1) IS MAN MORE THAN MATTER?

DOES death end all? Bound up inseparably with this question is another, viz., Is man more than matter? If we answer the latter question in the negative, we are naturally and inevitably driven to the conclusion that death is the end of us, and that there is no continuance or survival of our personality or any part of it once the last breath has left our bodies. Death then means extinction. This may be a consoling belief for some people, who find life a galling yoke, and who are quite content to lay down the burden of it and utterly cease to be. But it is not a belief that is compatible with a man's living his life at its highest and best. It lacks the dynamic force necessary for the creation of high ideals.

Before we can attempt to demonstrate that death does not end all, we must prove that man is more than matter. We must show that mind, the psyche, soul, or ego is not some material essence secreted by the brain, as the liver secretes bile, but is a separate entity.

If man is only matter, then all his thoughts, ambitions, ideals, hopes, and fears are nothing more than the outcome of some chemical, electrical, molecular, or other physical change in his brain cells. They become simply conditions of matter.

Let us think for a moment of our dearest friend. He has qualities of mind and character that attract and bind others to him. Are we to believe that his loyalty, his hopefulness, his sunny temperament, his honesty of purpose, his warmness of heart, his humour, his rare judgment, his gifts of imagination and of speech, and all those beauties of disposition and high qualities of mind that endear him to us, are nothing more than the outward expression of some subtle chemical or electrical changes in the grey matter of his brain?

Are the masterpieces of Titian and Raphael, the poems of Homer, Dante, and Milton, nothing more than effervescence in the brain cells transferred to canvas or to paper? The thing is unthinkable. We might as well declare that the smoke emitted from the funnel of a locomotive is the power which drives the train, or that the noise of a pistol shot propels the bullet, as believe that the physical changes in the brain cells are thought.

How can we imagine that alterations in our brain cells can determine moral issues? Can we write down conscience as nothing more than a chemical reaction in the test-tube of the brain? Is lofty and consecrated devotion to high ideals nothing more, let us say, than a hyperæmia of the brain, and must we attribute the reasoned self-sacrifice of Captain Oates to nothing higher than a physical cause. When that "gallant English gentleman" walked out from the lone tent into the Antarctic blizzard to die for his friends, was his noble act no more than the outward manifestation of a sluggishness of his intra-cranial blood-stream?

Let us face the question deliberately. If mind is nothing more than a function of the brain, the disintegration of the brain must necessarily mean that the mind perishes with that organ. On this point the materialist will seize with avidity. He will show that pathological processes in the brain are associated with alterations in the mind; that adhesions between the membranes of the brain and its surface, may produce mental and moral deterioration; that a tumour or other gross lesion in certain areas of the brain may reduce a man of the highest intellectual attainments to the level of a primitive bushman; that the presence of certain spiral micro-organisms in the grey matter may provoke the exalted ideas of the megalomaniac, or that the accumulation of fluid in the ventricles of the brain may convert a bright child into a gibbering idiot. He has a huge armoury of such facts, each of which, at a first glance, appears to be a formidable weapon; but his weightiest argument he keeps till the last, and he will assure us that we have absolutely no knowledge of mind apart from brain, and that for all practical purposes mind and brain are identical. But let us imagine that our materialist is a musician, and let us set him before a piano out of tune, with stiff keys and half a dozen broken wires, and, without telling him of the crippled condition of the instrument, let us ask him to play Beethoven's Moonlight Sonata. On such an instrument that exquisite harmony would become a discord. The player has all the necessary technical skill; the score is before his eyes, and his fingers touch the right keys at the right time. But the instrument is damaged; a hammer falls where there is no wire to catch its blow and tremble into music, and instead of a "concord of sweet sounds" we have chaotic dissonance. The analogy is a permissible one, and when the disgusted materialist rises from the instrument, we may point out to him that just as he has been unable to extract harmony from the damaged piano, so the mind cannot, or at least does not, play the harmony of life on the keyboard of a diseased brain.

The brain is the organ through which the mind expresses itself; it is the vehicle by which mind reveals itself; but we have no right to conclude that mind cannot and does not exist independently of, and apart from, the forty-odd ounces of nerve tissue that are aggregated in our skulls. Until a short time ago we did not know energy apart from matter. Matter is the vehicle through which energy expresses itself, or makes itself felt; but matter and energy are not identical. In the same way the brain and the mind are not identical, and a time may come when we shall be able to recognize mind when it reveals itself through some other medium than the brain. That this is not an extravagant dream is proved when we remember that science had no conception of energy apart from matter till it was compelled to presuppose the ether —that immaterial fabric which conveys the waves of solar energy from the sun to the earth. Now, in the gamma rays of radium, it has another proof that energy may express itself through other vehicles than matter. Science has had to wait long and patiently for this revelation, and the revelation has come, not as of old on the fire-capped peak of Sinai, in the law-giving voice of God, but as the reward of the patient, brilliant researches of a woman of genius in a laboratory in Paris.

Let us admit that we do not at present know mind apart from brain. Our ignorance does not rule such a possibility out of court. Endowed though we may be with great gifts of perception and marvellous capabilities of sensation, our perceptual capacities are very limited, and our senses often deceive us. In the lonely recesses of some remote mountain we may be impressed by the intense stillness and quietness that pervade the solitude, but, if our ears were tuned to hear, we should perceive that the whole earth and air are vocal with sounds that are lost to us because our auditory apparatus is able to capture sounds only of a certain pitch. In the same way, though vision is one of our most wonderful possessions, we are little more than blind men groping our way with tapping-sticks along the pathway of life, catching but vague and uncertain glimpses of the world in which we live. There are things around us that we cannot see; there are sounds that we cannot hear; but our inability to perceive them does not wipe them out of being. So we have no right to conclude that mind or soul cannot persist apart from brain because as yet we are unable to demonstrate their separate existence.

The materialist will tell us that thought, consciousness, and all the attributes of mind are nothing more than products of the brain. But there is another point of view: and it is not impossible that, far from producing thought and consciousness, the brain may actually limit them, and confine them within its own narrow compass.

Let us imagine that we are sitting in a closed and darkened room, with only a faint beam of light struggling through the curtain that covers the window. When the curtain is thrown back, the light can enter the room, and the amount which will come through the window—the intensity of the source remaining the same—will depend on the character of the glass that fills it. Clear glass will let through much more light than opaque glass, and a large window will admit more light than a couple of tiny panes. So it may be with the stream of consciousness. The clear window of the brain of a normal healthy man will admit more consciousness than the nerve ganglia of one of the lower vertebrates. And just as the rose window of some ancient cathedral will break up the beams of light that penetrate it into shafts of gold, and ruby red, and blue, letting them fall in a cascade of beauty on the pavement between the choir-stalls, so the stream of consciousness flowing through the brain of a poet or a man of genius will produce a more brilliant result than when it flows through the cottage window of some peasant's brain. It is not given to all of us to live behind "rose windows." Most of us have to be content with more commonplace illumination. But when we escape from our cathedral or our cottage, though we leave the windows behind we do not leave the light; but discover that we have emerged into an effulgence of illumination of which our little windows gave us no idea. As the windows limit our light, so our brains may limit our consciousness. The glass does not create the light, it simply transmits it, modifying it in accordance with its own qualities. It is, therefore, more than possible that our brain, instead of creating consciousness, only modifies, according to its own inherent quality, the rays of consciousness that play upon it. Light is not recognized as such till it impinges upon the retina and is transmitted by the optic nerve to the visual centre. So, it may be, we are aware of consciousness only through the action of some subtle influence outside ourselves playing upon our brain.

We may burn our cathedral and shatter all its glass; we may raze our little cottage to the ground; but we cannot, by so doing, destroy the light that filled them. And so, though we may destroy the body and the brain of a man, his mind or psyche is beyond our reach, as elusive and as impalpable as the ether.

We live in a day when the tendency is to believe nothing except what is capable of scientific proof, and there are many men who will not accept as a fact anything which they cannot "verify." The attitude of mind is honest, but it is unreasonable. Let us admit at once that we cannot demonstrate the existence of the mind, or soul, or ego, as a separate entity by scientific methods. The instruments of science are material, they cannot weigh, or analyse, or measure the immaterial. But the beliefs which cannot be established on a verifiable basis of fact to-day are often the truisms of to-morrow. The pseudo-science of the barber's shop or the raucous orator at the street corner is not the science of the laboratory. Many eminent men of science are quite content to believe where they cannot prove, and the truly great scientific investigator is usually a man of reverent mind. A Paine or a Strindberg will deny, where a Kelvin or a Lister will keep silence in reverent expectancy.

Archimedes had never dreamed, and could not prove, that our globe travels round the sun; but the earth rolled on in its orbit unperturbed. If someone had whispered to Sir Isaac Newton some hint of the marvels of radio-activity, we can imagine that he would have hesitated to believe them, for in his day science had not discovered the means of verifying such facts. But radium and uranium and thorium existed before Sir Isaac was born, and the fact that they and their peculiar properties had not been discovered did not put them out of existence. The forces which carry a message across the Atlantic through the ether have existed from the beginning of time, but they were not recognized and harnessed for our use till Marconi made his wonderful discovery.

Because, therefore, we cannot by scientific methods demonstrate the existence of mind apart from brain we have no scientific warrant to deny its possibility. Some day, perhaps, proof may be possible, but the time is not yet. Only a generation ago there seemed to be an impassable gulf between physics and metaphysics. Now physics is becoming more metaphysical, and is hesitating with uncertain foot on the lower steps of

"The great world's altar-stairs
That slope through darkness up to God."

CHAPTER IX

DOES DEATH END ALL?
(2) THE SURVIVAL OF PERSONALITY

"Man that is born of a woman is of few days, and full of trouble. He cometh forth like a flower, and is cut down . . .

"If a man die, shall he live again?"

JOB, chapter xiv.

"Non omnis moriar: multaque pars mei,
   Vitabit Libitinam."

HORACE.

"There are no dead."

MAETERLINCK (*The Blue Bird*).

"Thou wilt not leave us in the dust:
   Thou madest man, he knows not why,
   He thinks he was not made to die
And Thou hast made him: Thou art just."

TENNYSON.

"Because I love this life, I know I shall love death as well. The child cries out when from the right breast the mother takes it away, in the very next moment to find in the left one its consolation."

RABINDRANATH TAGORE.

CHAPTER IX

DOES DEATH END ALL? (2) THE SURVIVAL OF PERSONALITY

In the preceding chapter we have seen that the facts of life cannot be adequately explained on a materialistic basis. Man is something more than matter. He is matter knit with mind. He represents a symbiosis of body and soul, of living tissues and "personality." Will his personality survive the shock of the death of the body? I believe it will.

We shall best arrive at a satisfactory answer to this question if we begin by considering a few elementary properties of matter and energy.

It is a fundamental fact of physical science that matter is indestructible. It may change its form, but it cannot be destroyed, and, so far, has never been created by human agency. The clouds that sail majestically through the ether were but a few short days ago part of the opulent bosom of the sea. That subtle chemist, the Sun, playing his beams upon river and ocean has converted some of the water into vapour, which is borne aloft and aggregated into the cloud masses that sweep like white-rigged galleons across the sky. In their wind-driven courses they come into touch with the cool atmosphere of the hill-tops, and discharge their burden of vapour in the form of rain. The rain feeds the rivers, and the rivers feed the sea, and the unending cycle repeats itself as it has from the beginning of the world.

A great flake of blue-grey ash falls from a smoker's cigar, and soon there will be nothing left but a heap of dust and a sodden stump. But the matter that constituted the cigar still persists. It has only changed its form. Some of it has been converted into heat; some has floated into the atmosphere as ghostly coils of smoke; some has gone to make the perfume and aroma that have soothed the smoker; some lies in the heap of ash. The cigar has ceased to be; but the matter which constituted it all persists, though it is past the wit of the wisest chemist to synthetize these separated particles and reconstruct it again.

I look out of my window and see a cloud of dust caught up from the tawny surface of the road by the April wind. It sweeps over the hedges and falls on the fields, which are already carpeted with fresh green. The dust consists of the waste products of animal life, and of an infinite number of fine particles worn off the surface of the road from stone, and rock, and beaten earth by the trafficking feet of wayfaring men. It falls upon the pastures. It is lowly dust, so lowly that many feet have trodden upon it, but it has suddenly been called to the higher services of nature. It lies like some grey filmy vesture on the grass and the young sprouting crops. Then comes the gentle benediction of the rain, and the dust enters upon a new life. It is carried down into the earth, where the seeking rootlets await it. It yields itself to them, gives up whatever nourishment it contains, and becomes a part of the scarlet poppy or the golden corn, or the no less useful grass of the field. What was once dishonoured dust has been used for the upbuilding of food for men and cattle, and in due time some of it will become part of the human body. Our brains, the cunning instruments of our mind, are housed in by walls of bone which contain salts that may once have been a handful of dust blown from a wind-swept road.

It is a startling but incontrovertible fact that all the elements which went to make up the garment of flesh that was the earthly tabernacle of Julius Cæsar, and that every atom that, by its orderly and harmonious arrangement, constituted the beautiful and seductive body of Cleopatra are still in existence somewhere in the universe. Changed they may be, but they still persist; and infinitesimal particles that once were a part of Cleopatra may now be enshrined in the pure beauty of some lily of the Nile, or in the dusky loveliness of some daughter of the Egyptian desert. This is not transmigration of the soul, nor reincarnation. It is nothing more than a restatement of the fact that matter is indestructible, and that though it may change its character or its surroundings it still persists, and may be used again, as a builder may use an old brick, in the construction of a body similar to that of which it once formed a constituent part. Examples of the kind might be multiplied indefinitely, but enough has been said to illustrate the point and to show that matter cannot be destroyed.

Side by side with this elementary fact of physical science there is another, namely, the conservation of energy.

When a cue strikes a billiard-ball, some of the force expended by the muscles of the driving arm is used to overcome the inertia of the stationary ball; some of the energy gives it momentum, which is given up in turn to overcome the friction of the surface of the table and the resistance of the air, and finally much of the energy is given up when the ball strikes the resilient cushion, or cannons against another ball to which it transfers a considerable portion of the energy it has carried from the muscles of the player. Now if all the heat, and movement of the atmosphere, and the amount of force expended by the ball in impinging on the cushion or in striking the other ball, could be collected and converted again into the same kind of energy, and measured by a suitable machine, it would be found to equal exactly the amount of energy which the player expended when he struck the ball. Energy tends to become dissipated and altered in character, but its amount in the universe is constant.

Let us take another commonplace example. Thousands of years ago the sun shone on primeval forests in our land, and the leaves of the trees caught its generous rays and locked them up in their hearts. Ages have passed; the forests have disappeared and are hidden in the form of coal under many feet of earth. But men have sought out these buried repositories of solar energy, and when we warm ourselves before a blazing fire or annihilate distance in an express train, we are making use of the stored-up heat and light that left the sun myriads of years ago, and that has been hidden as potential energy since the days when the young leaves first spread themselves. It is a strange paradox, but industrial England, with all its gloom and smoke, is built on sunbeams.

Matter and energy cannot be destroyed. Now man has not created matter, nor can he create energy, but he can control both. He can change the form of matter by making use of accumulated experience. He can lessen the dissipation of energy by transferring it into useful channels; he can, by the reasoned use of his knowledge, lock up by chemical combinations an infinite amount of potential energy in such a substance as dynamite, or in our most modern explosive, trinitrotoluol, and he is able to convert the potential energy in a stream of water from an Alpine glacier into electrical energy which will propel a train to the top of a mountain. Matter and energy are his servants; not the servants of his physical body, but of his intellect or mind. The servants are indestructible; shall the master be destroyed? Surely, Reason can make but one answer, which is that mind also is imperishable and must persist.

Still another argument may be advanced, from the physical side, to support the idea of the survival of the soul or mind. Human life consists of two forms of life progressing simultaneously. There is the vegetative life of the cells out of which the body is built, and there is the conscious life of the ego. Until a few years ago it was believed that a part of the body removed by operation lost its vitality immediately or very shortly after its separation from the body proper. But we live in an era of great discoveries. Almost every day some trifle of flotsam or jetsam is pulled out of the ocean of knowledge, and it has been discovered that, under suitable conditions, parts of the body, and even whole organs taken from it, will continue to live for long periods after their removal

A Russian physiologist has shown that the human heart will continue to contract with a normal rhythm, many hours after its removal from the body; while French and American surgeons have shown that parts of the body may be removed and kept alive for prolonged periods, and may, at a later date, be transplanted or regrafted into other bodies, where they will once again resume their normal functions. Some of these tissues, in suitable media, will actually continue to grow for a period after their separation from the body. Now, if these things are true of the merely vegetative life of man, surely we have reasonable ground for believing that the conscious life of the ego, a thing infinitely higher than the vegetative life of the cell, will continue after its separation from the body. It is straining our credulity to believe that what has been proved, by scientific experiment, to be true of the lower shall not also be true of the higher.

There are some who are willing to admit that death does not mean annihilation, but who hesitate to accept the possibility of the mind or soul surviving as a definite personality. They are prepared to go so far as to allow that, at death, a spiritual something may leave the body, and merge at once into some great central source of soul, losing its identity in the infinite. This, however, would not mean the survival of the soul as an ego, and I do not accept the theory. I am persuaded that the soul persists as personality, and does not change into some lower form of "energy," blown upon by every vagrant wind that frolics between the stars. It persists as personality with this essential difference, that it is freed from the trammels and limitations of the physical body.

It does not lose its identity, like the water of a bottle opened in the depths of the sea, or like air that escapes into the surrounding atmosphere from a deflated tyre. It remains a separate entity; it persists as an ego.

In support of this opinion we may adduce the following facts. Behind all nature there is law. No sensible man to-day imagines that this earth of ours is a wandering fragment of matter tossed into infinite space. The mind of man has discovered that its movements are governed by certain laws; that all the regular phenomena of nature, the succession of day and night, the seasons, the tides, the movement of the planets, are all subject to laws. Now man has discovered many of these laws. He has given them concrete expression. He did not make them, though he makes deductions from them, and orders his life on the grounded belief that the law of nature in operation yesterday will still be in force on the morrow. He has deciphered them, as they were written in imperishable characters on the pages of nature by the great First Cause. They are rational laws, so we take it that they are the work of a First Cause that is not some blind force, but that is rational or that has reason. And it is man's proudest boast that he is a rational being, that he too has reason.

Now, we cannot imagine that the great First Cause was driven by any outside compulsion to create the Universe. It was the outcome of an act of free will; and man is a free agent—he, too, has free will. So that man, this infinitesimal speck in the Universe, this mere ant busying himself with his daily cares on his little ant-heap, has some of the attributes of the divine, the eternal and unchangeable. And these attributes must persist as they are. Reason cannot be degraded into some form of energy, and Will cannot be dissipated into heat. They must persist as a part of our personality.

We may, however, seek proof of the probability of the survival of man's personality in many other directions. Since man's appearance upon the earth, no other question has had such a perennial interest for him; no problem has tormented him with such anxieties; and the solution of no other enigma has been sought after with such unconquerable hope. The universality of the belief that man is an immortal soul is in itself some proof of the assumption. The hope of immortality is a basic fact in most religions, and a dominant keynote, and an assured conviction of Christianity, the loftiest of all.

In the priceless volumes of *The Golden Bough*, Sir James Frazer has accumulated evidence to prove that the belief in the existence of a soul, which survives separation from the body, is shared by many primitive peoples. Naturally, the ideas of primitive peoples vary as to the nature, the functions, the attributes, and the fate of the soul, and are not to be compared with the sublime psychology of the Christian religion. We must, however, distinguish between the existence of a belief, and the particular form in which that belief may express itself. The important point is that the belief is widespread, and any belief that is widely distributed among scattered peoples, between whom there can have been no contact, is entitled to consideration.

This belief or hope had its birth very early in the history of the human race. Palæolithic man buried with his dead weapons and implements which he believed would be of service in the life beyond the tomb. It was held by the ancient Egyptians, who had elaborated an eschatology of their own in which Osiris judged the souls of the dead. We catch vague whisperings of it in the deathless verses of the Greek poets; but it culminated in Hellenic philosophy in the person of Socrates, who drank his cup of hemlock with the confident assurance that it could only destroy his body, but would leave Socrates, the soul, untouched, free to depart "into that invisible region which is of its own nature, the region of the divine, the immortal, the wise." Since the days of Plato this problem of immortality has been one of the chief rallying grounds of the philosophers, and the arguments that have been suggested by way of proof are almost incalculable in number.

Philosophy and religion alike have laid stress upon the incompleteness of life, and have based upon that a hope for the continuance of personality after death. The best and fullest life falls far short of its ideals and aspirations. It is nothing more than an arc of a great circle, whose circumference can only be completed in the beyond.

The loftier a man's ideals, the less opportunity is there of seeing their attainment in this life. "The man with the muckrake" can get out of life all that he seeks after; the pure soul of a Sir Galahad, with ideas of absolute truth and absolute goodness, cannot attain its goal this side of the grave. If there is any justice in the scheme of things, as we know there is, surely the high ideal will not be penalized.

Then, further, a means of satisfaction has been provided for every longing of which the human being is capable. If he hunger and thirst, there is food and drink in abundance for the satisfaction of these primitive instincts. If he is weary there is

"Tired Nature's sweet restorer, balmy sleep."

If he long for beauty, the whole panorama of nature unrolls itself before his wondering eyes, and in the glory of the setting sun, the grey grandeur of wave-swept rocks, the perfect form of the lowliest flower of the field, or the majesty of a starlit night, his longing for the beautiful is satisfied. Or does he love and long for harmony? Let him listen to the twice-sung melody of the thrush; let him lend an ear to the aspiring and invisible skylark; let him hearken to the babbling of the tinkling brook, the whisper of the wind or the diapason of the sea. Does he glory in his strength? The lofty peak of the mountain challenges him to the ascent; and the heaving waves of the ocean cry to be cleft by the swimmer's arm. And even when many of the ordinary avenues of sense are closed, the longings, and aspirations, and desires of the soul behind the barred windows can still be satisfied. To read the marvellous stories of Helen Keller, who, at the age of nineteen months, became deaf, dumb, and blind, or of Marthe and Marie Heurtin of Poitou, who were born deaf, dumb, and blind, is to learn how beings apparently isolated, except by the sense of touch, from all the wonder of the outside world can still be made able to communicate with others, and to enjoy and participate in the fuller life around them. Surely we have a right to anticipate that, if provision has been made for gratifying all the ordinary desires of the human heart, this lofty aspiration for continued life after death shall not fail of its fulfilment. Is it to be the only longing that is unsatisfied? As Adam Ferguson has said, "The desire for immortality is an instinct, and can reasonably be regarded as an indication of that which the Author of this desire wills to do."

A nebulous immortality, in which we are not to be conscious of our personal identity, but in which we are to be degraded into some lower form of "energy" would not be the answer to the instinctive longings we feel stirring in our breasts.

Life at every stage is a probation. The unborn infant is daily gaining strength to prepare it ultimately for its issue into the world. If it could think and reason during the long months of its pre-natal existence it might imagine that the life of which it has experience is the only life it will ever enjoy, and that the cataclysm of birth will mean for it annihilation. In the fullness of time it emerges into a world more wonderful and more beautiful than anything it ever dreamed of, an experience for which the previous months of its existence have been nothing more than a preparation. The sheltered years of infancy and childhood are a preparation for the joyous adventure of youth. The solstice of youth is a preparation for the fruition of manhood and womanhood; and the opulent days of manhood are a preparation for the reflective calm of old age. All through life, from its earliest dawn, each successive stage is a preparation and period of probation for the stage that is immediately to succeed it. No period of life is its own fulfilment, each stage is preparatory to the next. It is, therefore, altogether unlikely that this rule of life will break down at the end, and that the strenuous days a man has lived, the knowledge he has won, the character he has hammered out for himself on the anvil of experience, the personality he has built up, will go for nothing, and that the purpose of life is fulfilled by the year or two of tremulous senescence in which it often culminates. To believe this is to stultify ourselves. All life is a probation, and, beyond the barrier of death, I am confident that there awaits us a world as wonderful and as little dreamed of as that which awaits the unborn child beyond the gate of birth.

"There is no death! What seems so is transition:
    This life of mortal breath
Is but a suburb of the life Elysian
    Whose portal we call Death."

I think there is much to be said for the argument in favour of the survival of personality based by the theologians on the existence of conscience. The promptings of conscience are something more than mere lip-service to the conventionally recognized standard of conduct. It is not a product of education, though a wise education, properly perfused and interpenetrated by religious teaching, will impart an added sensibility to the conscience. Without conscience, society would degenerate into anarchy. Laws alone will not restrain the wild passions of man, and when out of reach of the law he would, but for conscience, tend rapidly to degenerate to the level of the brutes. Conscience controls the ruler as well as the ruled. It is "the still small voice" in the heart of man, and it operates by reminding us that we are in some measure answerable for all our deeds, if not to the tribunal of public opinion, to the higher assize in the life hereafter. And it is this knowledge, derived from the whisperings of conscience, and held firmly by many simple folks who could not give any very valid reason for their belief in a future life, that has saved the world from being given over to the unbridled passions of mankind.

When all is said, we have to admit that the arguments for the survival of personality are infinitely more weighty than any that can be adduced against it. The opponents of immortality have nothing but negative evidence to support their position, and in science the negative argument is valueless. It may be hard, and probably many people find it very hard to believe that their personality will continue after death; but it is harder still for them to imagine their own extinction. There is something within us which rebels against the thought, and that something is the soul's consciousness of its own immortal destiny.

It has been suggested that personality cannot persist because memory is one of the first faculties of the mind to fail; and without memory, it is urged, personality cannot be continuous. But those who advance this argument forget that there is a subconscious memory, in which would seem to be buried all the incidents and experiences of the past. This subconscious memory may be stirred into activity in conditions of artificially produced hypnosis, and sometimes gives startling manifestations of its existence in the senile and the dying, who suddenly recall, with perfect accuracy, events that have happened in the days of their earliest childhood. Goethe has put on record a remarkable instance of this, in the case of an old peasant who, on his death-bed, suddenly declaimed several passages in the most classical Greek. It was generally believed that the old man did not know a single word of Greek, but on a careful investigation being made, it was discovered that when a boy he had been compelled to commit to memory and to repeat certain Greek passages to stimulate to emulation an aristocratic dunce. In this way he had acquired a mechanical knowledge of Greek phraseology. He never knew the meaning of the words; but they remained, accurately deposited in his subconscious memory, until their unexpected repetition, many years afterwards, surprised the watchers by his bed. The subconscious memory seems to be immune against the ravages of time; and it is probable that it will serve to supply the personality with all the memories necessary for its continuance as a separate identity.

No valid argument against the survival of personality can be deduced from the fact that the dead are silent, and do not communicate with those they have left behind. When, as frequently happens, we are "cut off" from a friend with whom we are talking on the telephone, the abrupt ending of the conversation does not mean that one or other of us has ceased to be. It simply indicates that, for the time being, the means of communication between us has been interrupted.

I do not venture to base any conclusion

as to the survival of personality upon the so-called results of psychical research. There are earnest men, and men of scientific eminence, who claim to have been in personal communication with the spirits of the departed, and to have received messages from them. But any evidence which I have examined has left me unconvinced. At most these so-called messages amount to little more than vague and incoherent babblings, or to crazy scribblings on a slate.

It is reasonable to suppose that if the spirit of a Gladstone or a Myers or a Stead could communicate with those who have sought to reach them from this side of the "great gulf fixed," the message given would be something worthy of the men—some trumpet-tongued revelation for the times, some brave word of encouragement for those who are still entangled in the meshes of life. But, instead, any communication has been little more than the unconnected rambling of some idiot boy. Some day, perhaps, those who love to grope with blind fingers along the edge of this gulf of separation may stumble upon some great discovery, and may get into touch with those who have passed onward. But the time is not yet.

It is altogether outside my province to discuss the fate of the soul after its survival of the shock of death. On this matter the battle is still raging in the camp of the theologians, and where the doctors of divinity are still at variance it would be supreme effrontery for a mere doctor of medicine to obtrude his views. But my reticence to touch on this point is not the outcome of any invertebrate belief. Science has nothing to do with eschatology. My thesis has been to show that there is nothing inherently impossible in the survival of personality. Absolute proof is as yet beyond our reach, but I am persuaded that even without the inspiring assurances of revealed religion, which in this matter must be the *ultima ratio* of all thinking men, we have good grounds to comfort ourselves with hope. As Emerson says, "I am a better believer, and all serious souls are better believers in immortality than we can give grounds for. The real evidence is too subtle, or is higher than we can write down in propositions. We cannot prove our faith by syllogisms."

In what is, perhaps, the most perfect Petrarchan sonnet in our language, Blanco White has given permanent expression to this stupendous problem of Life and Death which has always vexed mankind. He imagines our first parent seized by a paroxysm of awe when he learns that day will wane, and be succeeded by the mystery of night. Black night, dark and inscrutable! What will become of his beautiful Eden swathed in impenetrable gloom? But Night comes, bringing with her no hideous mystery, but a miracle of revelation. So death itself may wake us from the sleep of life to a knowledge vaster, grander, and more sublime than anything we have ever dreamed of.

"Mysterious Night, when our first parent knew
Thee from report divine, and heard thy name,
Did he not tremble for this lovely frame,
This glorious canopy of light and blue?
Yet, 'neath a curtain of translucent dew,
  Bathed in the rays of the great setting flame,
  Hesperus with the hosts of Heaven came,
And lo! Creation widened in man's view.

"Who could have thought such darkness lay concealed
  Within thy beams, O Sun! or who could find,
Whilst flower and leaf and insect stood revealed,
  That to such countless orbs thou mad'st us blind!
Why do we then shun Death with anxious strife?
If Light can thus deceive, wherefore not Life?"

CHAPTER X
EPILOGUE

"Morte carent animæ: semperque priore relicta
Sede, novis habitant domibus vivuntque receptæ."

OVID.

"Measure thy life by loss instead of gain;
Not by the wine drunk, but the wine poured forth;
For love's strength standeth in love's sacrifice;
And whoso suffers most hath most to give."

HARRIET E. H. KING.

"Peace, let it be! for I loved him, and love him forever:
The dead are not dead, but alive."

TENNYSON.

CHAPTER X

EPILOGUE

We have already learned some lessons from the world-war that still rages: lessons in strategy, in military tactics, in economics, in national organization, in finance. But there are other lessons we are learning, for in our history is being repeated the experience of the ancient taskmasters of Israel, when "there was a great cry in Egypt; for there was not a house where there was not one dead." So it has come to pass that men's thoughts are daily turned to the contemplation of death, which has ceased to be regarded as a thing remote and improbable, and has become a recognized incident in our daily lives. And the recognition of the fact of death has directed our thoughts afresh to the problem of immortality, and it is no exaggeration to say that many thousands of people, who two years ago had but the most ill-defined ideas as to the survival of personality, are to-day firmly convinced that life is continued beyond the barrier of death.

Faith has led boldly, where Reason felt constrained to grope, and sometimes the human heart is a surer guide than the human head. Heart and mind alike refuse to believe that the brave little midshipmen, in the first flower of their youth, whose bodies now lie fathoms deep in the waters of the Southern Pacific or the North Sea, have passed into nothingness. They had so much to give; they gave it gladly; they gave it all. For such altruism is there no reward? Are these brave boys, and the many thousands more whose life-blood has poured into the soil of Flanders, or on the sands of the Ægean Sea, to be penalized for their bravery in defence of the right, while the self-indulgent gourmand, who hides behind his fatty heart—the result of his own vices—which protects him from being called upon for service, extracts out of life every ounce of enjoyment it can offer? It is quite impossible to believe that such obvious unfairness can satisfy the demands of ordinary justice. But, unless there is a life beyond the grave, there is no assize which can readjust the inequality.

Love demands the immortality of those whom she has lost; and Love knows that she does not ask in vain. A mother who has lost her only son, or the young wife whose "bridal garland falls upon the bier," may have had vague and shadowy ideas as to immortality before the thunder-cloud of calamity burst over them. But to many, suffering has brought revelation; and the veil that separates them from the Beyond has ceased to be an impenetrable curtain of black darkness, and has become as transparent as a drop of dew.

What they once hoped for weakly, they now know and believe with the full strength of their love; for they have heard, as once on a time another company of mourners heard, the voice of Him who overcame Death saying:

οὐκ ἀπέθανεν, ἀλλὰ καθεύδει.

He is not dead, but sleepeth.

INDEX

A

Adam, Dr., last words of, 74
Adanson's Baobab tree, 12
Addison, on death of Sir Thomas More, 68
Animals and death, 27
Argyll, Marquis of, execution of, 56
Auto-intoxication and sleep, 19
Average length of life, 13

B

Bacillus Bulgaricus, 15
Battle, bravery in, 42
—— excitement of, and death, 34
—— painlessness of wounds in heat of, 45
—— sensations in, 36 *et seq.*
Behring and Roux, diphtheritic antitoxin, 52
Benson, A. C., quoted, 64
—— on John Sterling's testimony, 73
—— a personal escape from death, 81
Bernard, Claude, 16
Boleyn, Anne, execution of, 68
Boswell on death, 66
Brain, and mind, the connection of, 143
—— the, an organ of mind, 146
—— the, as a railway terminus, 44
Bravery in battle, 42, 43
Brodie, Sir Benjamin, on fear of death, 83
Brontë, Charlotte, death of, 93
—— Emily, lines on death, 140
Browne, Sir Thomas, on sleep, 29
Browning, Robert, quoted, 128
Bryant, William Cullen, on death, 64; quoted, 135

C

Cæsar and Cleopatra: their atoms still in existence, 160-161
Child, a world without a, 132
Coal, and conservation of energy, 163
Collier, and explosion of shells, 41
Colton, thought on death, 96
Conscience, argument for immortality from, 177
Consciousness and light, analogy between, 149-150
Consumptives' hope, 76
Cowper on suicide, 104
Cranmer, martyrdom of, 59-60
Cromwell, Oliver, last words of, 72
Crothers, S. McChord, quoted, 140

D

Damien, Father, 56
Darwin, Charles, last words of, 72
Dead, communications with the, 181
Death, a sleep and a forgetting, 86
—— and faith, 55
—— and life, Weismann on, 11
—— and love, 133
—— and physical pain, 99
—— and science, 10
—— and sleep, 28, 108-110
—— and the call of duty, 48
—— and the sleep of life, 183
—— animals and, 27
—— definition of, 20
—— dignity of, 21
—— drowning and the fear of, 80
—— faith overcoming fear of, 57
—— fear of, 27, 31, 36
—— fear of, and normal man, 65
—— fear of, Dr. Johnson's, 66
—— fear of, doctors and, 51
—— fear of, nurses and, 51
—— from capital punishment, 86
—— from drowning, 103
—— from old age, 18
—— gloom of, 33

Index

Death—*Continued*
—— inevitability of, 3-5, 20
—— instincts and emotions strengthened by, 131
—— loneliness of, 21
—— molecular, 16-17
—— no agony in, 114
—— no terror for the dying, 64
—— our daily contemplation of, 187
—— pain no part of, 102, 103
—— personality, survival of, after, 157
—— progress due to, 130
—— Sir Walter Raleigh on, 8, 70
—— soldiers and, 35
—— sudden, 110
—— the agony of, 117
—— the liberator, 135
—— the maternal instinct and fear of, 60
—— the moment of, 107
—— the philosophers and, 9
—— the scavenger, 136
—— what life gains from, 129
Die, reluctance to, 89-91
Dignity of death, 21
Diogenes the Epicurean, quoted, 96
Disharmonies of life, 27
Disraeli, Isaac, on death of Raleigh, 70
Doctors, duty of, in fatal diseases, 123
—— and euthanasia, 119
—— and fear of death, 44
—— experience of, with death, 74
Donne, quoted, 28, 29
Drowning, and fear of death, 80
—— deaths from, 103
Dust, an epic of the, 159
Duty, the call of, and fear of death, 48
Dying, care of the, 125
—— death no terror to the, 64

E

Ego of man, the, 142
Egyptians and souls of the dead, 170
Eliot, George, quoted, 133

Elixir of life, 15
Emerson, belief of, in immortality, 183
Energy, conservation of, 161
Epilepsy and pain, 100
Euthanasia, 117

F

Faith and death, 56, 188
Fear of death, 27, 31, 36
—— not an instinct, 34
—— not inborn, 29
Ferguson, Adam, quoted, 174
Finot and the fear of death, 31
Frazer, Sir James, *The Golden Bough*, 169

G

Goodhart, Sir J. F., on the fear of death, 85
Gull, Sir William, on death, 107
Guthrie, James, on fear of death, 58

H

Hazlitt, William, quoted, 26
Hegesias, 30
Holmes, Thomas, on conduct of murderers, 88
Hood, Thomas, quoted, 108, 109
Horace, quoted, 156
Hunter, Dr. William, last words of, 96, 107
Hypnotism, and the subconscious memory, 179

I

Immortality, the desire for, an instinct, 173
—— the universal hope of, 169

J

Jackson, Dr. A. F., death of, from plague, 54
Job, quoted, 156
Johnson, Dr. Samuel, and his fear of death, 66

K

Keats, John, quoted, 116
Keyser, Cassius J., quoted, 128
King, Harriet E. H., quoted, 186
Kingsley, Charles, in death, 22

L

Latimer, martyrdom of, 59
Length of life, average, 13
—— useful, 14
Life, a probation, 174–176
—— gains from death, what, 129
—— prolongation of, 15
—— the disharmonies of, 27
—— vegetative and conscious, 164
Light and consciousness, analogy between, 149–150
Lightning, death from, 106
Livingstone, Dr., and the lion, 81
Loneliness of death, 21
Longfellow, quoted, 135
Love and death, 133, 189

M

Mackail, Hugh, martyrdom of, 58
Macnaghten, Sir M. L., anecdote by, 87
Maeterlinck, 120; quoted, 156
Man more than matter, 141
Mankind, influence of death on history of, 134
Mary II., Queen, last words of, 72
Maternal instinct and fear of death, 60
Matter and energy servants of mind, 164
Metchnikoff, Professor Elie, and problem of prolonging life, 15; death, 16
Memory, the subconscious, 179
Milton's death, 111
Mind and brain, the connection of, 143
Molecular death, 17
Moment of death, the, 107
Momerie, Professor, on mental life, 140

Montaigne quoted, 2, 26, 85
More, Sir Thomas, execution of, 68
Müller, Dr. Hermann, death of, 53
Müller, Max, on Kingsley in death, 22

O

Oates, Captain, self-sacrifice of, 144
Old age, death from, 19
Osler, Sir William, on fear of death, 86
Ovid, quoted, 186

P

Paget, Sir James, on death, 107
Pain, no part of death, 102, 103
Parr, Thomas, age of, 13
Personality, after death, 157
—— reason and will part of, 169
—— survival of, 141 et seq.
—— soul persists as definite, 166
Physical pain and death, 99
Plato and immortality, 171
Pope, Alexander, death of, 111
Protozoa, immortality of the, 11
Psychical research, and communications with the dead, 181
Publius Lochius Syrus, quoted, 116

R

Raleigh, Sir Walter, quoted, 8
Rhodes, Cecil, last words of, 74
Ridley, martyrdom of, 59
Robertson of Brighton, quoted, 21
Rousseau and death, 28

S

Science and death, 10
Scott, Captain, death of, 73
—— last words of, 91
Seneca quoted, 2, 26
Shakespeare quoted, 26, 30

Sleep and death, 19, 28, 108–110
Smith, Alexander, on majesty of death, 22
Socrates and the soul, 171
Soldiers and death, 36
Southey, on John Wesley, 113
St. Mungo, age of, 13
Sudden death, 110
Suicide, 29

T

Tagore, Rabindranath, quoted, 156
Tennyson quoted, 106, 156, 186
Thought and consciousness, 149
Tolstoy and death, 28
Tyndall, 106

W

Weismann on life and death, 11
Wesley, Charles, death of, 112
Wesley, John, death of, 112, 113
White, Blanco, sonnet on Life and Death, 183–184
Whyte–Melville, quoted, 2
Wounds, painlessness of in heat of battle, 45

Y

Yeast fungus, 17
Younghusband, Sir Francis, experience of, 105

A Selection from the
Catalogue of

G. P. PUTNAM'S SONS

Complete Catalogues sent
on application

Continuity

By
Sir Oliver Lodge

$1.00 net. By mail, $1.10

The author contends against the tendency of the era apparent in the taking of refuge in vague forms of statement, the shrinking from close examination of the puzzling and obscure, and the denial of the existence of anything which makes no appeal to organs of sense—no ready response to laboratory experiment.

G. P. Putnam's Sons

New York London

The Argument against Materialism

Life and Matter

A Criticism of Professor Haeckel's
"A Riddle of the Universe"

By Sir Oliver Lodge

Crown 8vo. $1.00 net. By mail $1.10

The author fully acknowledges Haeckel's service to scientific thought in introducing Darwinism into Germany, and he admits that to advanced students Haeckel's writings can do nothing but good. He believes, however, that to some general readers they may do harm, unless accompanied by a suitable qualification or antidote, especially an antidote against the bigotry of their somewhat hasty and destructive portions.

"Deserves to rank with the best contributions by Huxley to scientific literature; while from the scientific standpoint it is timely in its appearance, brilliant in its conception, and admirable in execution. It should be welcomed by all who are interested in the development of true science, but who have no patience for blatant materialism. . . The utterance of a scientist eminent for his wonderful researches. . . . The book is full of interest and information."
Rev. James M. Owen, Lynchburg, Va.

"A fascinating reply to Haeckel's materialistic philosophy of life. The arguments are sane and sound. Lodge is a profound scientist, but he does not allow his scientific knowledge to obscure his general judgment."
Providence Journal.

New York—**G. P. Putnam's Sons**—London

Where No Fear Was

By

Arthur Christopher Benson

Author of "From a College Window," "The Upton Letters," etc.

12°. $1.50 net

In Mr. Benson's new book he turns for the reader many of the rich pages of his life. Yet the book is only incidentally autobiographical, the author drawing abundantly as well upon the great common hoard of experience for the portrayal and valuation of those fears, many of them tonic in their effect, which in a variety of forms goad man from infancy to old age. Fear, in the expansive sense in which Mr. Benson uses the term, is traced as an influence whether for good or for ill in the lives of Dr. Johnson, Tennyson, Ruskin, Carlyle, John Sterling, and Charlotte Brontë.

G. P. Putnam's Sons

New York   London

By Arthur Christopher Benson
Fellow of Magdalene College, Cambridge

Along the Road
12°. $1.50 net. By mail, $1.60

Mr. Benson's volume is a kind of jaunt along life's highway, a pleasing stretch of thoughts and sentiments. Many a tarrying place is found on the journey for meditation and comment on the values of things, or for the recalling of some impressive incident connected with the lives of great men of the past generation, many of whom were personally known to the author.

Joyous Gard
12°. $1.50 net. By mail, $1.60

Joyous Gard was the Castle of Sir Launcelot in the *Morte d'Arthur*, into which he retired, in the intervals of war and business, for rest and mirth. In the book called by this name the author pleads that many men and women could make for themselves a stronghold of the mind where they could follow according to their desire the track of things beautiful, intellectual, and spiritual, not from a sense of duty but for recreation and enjoyment, as a respite from daily work and trivial cares.

Watersprings
12°. $1.50 net. By mail, $1.60

A delicately conceived and thought-infused romance, the background of which is, for the most part, Cambridge University, among the scenes and associations of which the author's best years have been spent.

Where No Fear Was
12°. $1.50 net. By mail, $1.60

In this book the author turns for the reader many of the rich pages of his life. Yet the book is only incidentally autobiographical, he having drawn abundantly as well upon the great common hoard of experience for the portrayal and valuation of those fears, many of them tonic in their effect, which in a variety of forms goad man from infancy to old age.

New York   **G. P. Putnam's Sons**   **London**